I0013106

# ADVANCED ASSEMBLY LANGUAGE PROGRAMMING

Harnessing the Power of
Mnemonics and Optimized Machine
Code for High-Performance Systems

# NATHAN WESTWOOD

# TABLE OF CONTENTS

# ABOUT THE AUTHOR!

## Dr. Nathan Westwood

**Biography:**

Dr. Nathan Westwood is a pioneering technologist known for his exceptional contributions to the fields of software development, cloud computing, and artificial intelligence. With a passion for innovation and a relentless drive to solve complex problems, Nathan has become a prominent figure in the tech industry, shaping the future of digital technology.

Born and raised in Silicon Valley, Nathan's interest in technology started at a young age. His fascination with computers and coding led him to pursue a degree in Computer Science from Stanford University, where he excelled academically and honed his skills in programming and software engineering. During his time at Stanford, Nathan was involved in several cutting-edge projects that sparked his interest in AI and cloud technologies.

After graduating, Nathan joined a leading tech firm where he played a key role in developing cloud-based solutions that revolutionized data storage and analytics. His work in the early stages of cloud computing set the foundation for modern infrastructure-as-a-service (IaaS) platforms, earning him recognition as one of the industry's emerging stars. As a lead engineer, Nathan was instrumental in launching products that have since become industry standards.

Nathan's entrepreneurial spirit led him to co-found his own tech startup focused on AI-driven automation tools for businesses. Under his leadership, the company rapidly gained traction, attracting both investors and clients who were eager to leverage his innovative AI solutions to streamline operations and improve efficiency. Nathan's commitment to pushing the boundaries of what's possible in tech quickly earned him a reputation as a visionary leader.

Known for his expertise in machine learning, Nathan has also worked with several large tech companies, advising on the integration of AI and data science into their operations. His work has spanned various sectors, including healthcare, finance, and manufacturing, where he has helped organizations harness the power of data and automation to achieve exponential growth.

Beyond his technical achievements, Nathan is a sought-after speaker at global tech conferences, where he shares his insights on the future of cloud computing, artificial intelligence, and the ethical challenges posed by emerging technologies. His thought leadership and commitment to ethical innovation have made him a respected voice in the tech community.

In addition to his professional accomplishments, Nathan is deeply passionate about mentoring the next generation of tech leaders. He regularly contributes to educational programs and initiatives designed to inspire young minds and equip them with the skills necessary to thrive in the ever-evolving tech landscape.

Nathan Westwood continues to be a trailblazer in the tech industry, shaping the future of technology with his innovative ideas, entrepreneurial spirit, and commitment to making a positive impact on the world.

# CHAPTER 1:
# INTRODUCTION TO
# ASSEMBLY LANGUAGE

In the world of computing, many of us have become accustomed to using high-level languages such as Python, Java, or C++. These languages allow us to create complex software and systems, abstracting away the inner workings of the computer to make programming more accessible. However, beneath this level of abstraction lies the heart of every computing system—Assembly language.

While high-level languages are powerful and user-friendly, they are not the ultimate tool when it comes to squeezing every ounce of performance out of a system. That's where Assembly language comes in. Often seen as the realm of seasoned professionals or hobbyists looking to delve deeper into their hardware, Assembly is still a crucial skill, especially when dealing with performance-critical applications. In this chapter, we will explore the fundamentals of Assembly language, understand its historical significance, and explain why it remains relevant in today's high-performance computing landscape.

## Overview of Assembly Language

Assembly language is often referred to as a low-level programming language, but what exactly does that mean? At its core, Assembly is a symbolic representation of machine code, the language spoken by the computer's CPU. Unlike high-level programming languages, which are designed to be human-readable and abstract away hardware details, Assembly language operates close to the hardware level, allowing direct interaction with the computer's memory and CPU registers.

In Assembly, you won't be dealing with abstracted commands or simplified syntax. Instead, you'll be using mnemonics—short, symbolic names for instructions and operations that the CPU can execute directly. These mnemonics correspond to machine code instructions that the CPU understands. When you write Assembly code, you're essentially creating a program that the computer can understand at its most basic level.

But before we dive into how Assembly works in practice, let's take a look at its historical context and why it's still important today.

## Historical Context of Assembly Language

The history of Assembly language is intertwined with the early development of computers. In the beginning, computers were controlled by punch cards and switches, a far cry from the sophisticated operating systems and high-level programming languages we use today. The first generation of computers didn't have operating systems or programming languages like we know them. Instead, programmers would write machine code by manipulating binary numbers (0s and 1s) to control the hardware.

As computers evolved, so did the need for more efficient and readable programming methods. The earliest programming languages, such as machine code, were cumbersome and prone to errors, which made writing programs a time-consuming and error-ridden process. Enter Assembly language, which emerged as a human-readable intermediary between machine code and higher-level languages.

Assembly language revolutionized programming by providing a more understandable way to work with machine-level operations. Instead of manually dealing with binary numbers, programmers could use mnemonics that represented various machine instructions. For example, a simple operation like adding two numbers might be represented by the mnemonic ADD, making the code far more comprehensible than raw binary.

While Assembly provided a huge leap forward in making programming more accessible, it still retained the close relationship to the hardware that machine code provided. Assembly language didn't abstract away the details of the hardware; it simply made them more understandable and manageable.

Over time, higher-level programming languages such as FORTRAN, C, and later Python and Java, further abstracted away the underlying hardware details, making programming even more accessible. Despite this, Assembly language remained an essential tool for systems programming, embedded systems, performance optimization, and low-level hardware control.

## Why Assembly Remains Crucial in Modern High-Performance Computing

You may wonder, in an era dominated by high-level languages and sophisticated compilers, why would anyone still bother with Assembly language? The truth is, Assembly is still relevant today, particularly in situations where performance is paramount. While high-level languages are great for rapid development and general-purpose applications, they don't provide the fine-grained control over the hardware that Assembly does.

At the lowest levels, Assembly allows programmers to optimize code for speed, memory usage, and power consumption—key factors in performance-critical applications such as embedded systems, game development, operating system kernels, and real-time computing. In industries like aerospace, automotive, and medical devices, where systems must run at their absolute best, Assembly programming is still used to optimize performance to the maximum.

Moreover, Assembly allows direct manipulation of the CPU's registers and memory, which can be crucial for certain tasks like hardware control, device drivers, and low-level system utilities. Modern processors, like those used in smartphones, gaming consoles, and servers, are built with complex instruction sets (such as x86 or ARM) that support Assembly-level programming for more precise control.

By working with Assembly, developers can make use of specialized processor instructions, understand the interaction between memory and CPU, and even optimize their software to a level that high-level languages cannot achieve. This is why Assembly remains a powerful tool for developers who need to work with hardware directly or squeeze out every bit of performance from a system.

## Understanding Machine Language and Assembly

To truly understand Assembly language, it's essential to understand its relationship with machine language, also known as binary code. Machine language is the lowest-level programming language that the CPU can understand. It consists of binary instructions, typically represented as 1s and 0s, that tell the computer exactly what to do—add numbers, move data around, perform logical operations, etc.

However, writing in machine language is incredibly difficult for humans, which is where Assembly comes in. Assembly language acts as a symbolic representation of these machine code instructions, using mnemonics and labels to make the code more readable.

For example, consider an operation in machine code that might look like this:

```
10110000 01100001
```

This binary string might represent a command for the CPU to load a value into a register. In Assembly, it could be represented as:

```
nginx
```

```
MOV AL, 61h
```

Here, MOV is the mnemonic for the "move" instruction, and AL refers to a specific register. The value 61h is the hexadecimal representation of the number 97, which might be stored in that register. As you can see, Assembly language is much easier to understand and work with compared to raw machine code.

But how does this all tie into how computers actually execute these instructions? To answer that, we need to understand the basics of the CPU and memory architecture.

## The Basics of a CPU and Memory Architecture

The central processing unit (CPU) is the heart of any computer system. It's the component responsible for executing instructions, performing calculations, and managing data flow between various system components. The CPU is made up of several key parts, including the **ALU (Arithmetic Logic Unit)**, **registers**, and **control unit**.

In Assembly programming, one of the most important concepts to grasp is how the CPU executes instructions. Assembly language allows us to directly manipulate the CPU's registers—small, fast memory locations that hold data temporarily as the CPU processes it. Registers are used to store values like variables, pointers, and intermediate results during computation.

When a program is written in Assembly, it is a series of instructions that tell the CPU what to do, step by step. The CPU fetches each instruction from memory, decodes it, and then executes it. This is the fundamental process behind every computer operation, whether it's running a web browser or controlling a spacecraft.

When you write Assembly code, you are telling the CPU how to manipulate data directly within these registers and how to access data stored in memory. Understanding how the CPU interacts with memory and processes instructions is crucial for optimizing Assembly code.

## How Computers Execute Assembly Instructions

Now that we understand the relationship between Assembly and machine code, and the role of the CPU, let's look at how computers actually execute Assembly instructions.

When an Assembly program is compiled, the assembler converts the human-readable mnemonics into machine code, which the CPU can understand. The machine code consists of binary instructions that directly control the hardware.

Once the program is loaded into memory, the CPU begins executing the instructions, one by one, in a process called the **fetch-decode-execute cycle**. This cycle is repeated continuously as long as the program is running. The CPU fetches the next instruction from memory, decodes it to determine what action to perform, and then executes that action.

For example, consider an Assembly instruction that adds two numbers together:

```sql
ADD AX, BX
```

In this case, the ADD instruction tells the CPU to add the value in the BX register to the value in the AX register. After executing this instruction, the result of the addition is stored back in the AX register.

This is a simple example, but it illustrates how Assembly allows you to control the flow of data within the CPU and its registers. The more complex the operation, the more sophisticated the Assembly code will be, but the underlying principle remains the same: the CPU is executing instructions from memory, and those instructions tell the CPU how to manipulate data and perform tasks.

# Hands-On Project: Writing Your First Simple Assembly Program (Hello, World!)

Now that we've covered the theory, it's time to write your first Assembly program. In this hands-on project, you will write a simple "Hello, World!" program in Assembly language.

**Step 1: Setting Up Your Environment** Before you can write Assembly code, you need to set up a development environment. You'll need an assembler, such as NASM (Netwide Assembler), and a way to run your program, such as a Linux-based operating system or an emulator for your target architecture.

**Step 2: Writing the Code** The program we'll write will simply print "Hello, World!" to the screen. Here's the basic code for the program:

```assembly
section .data
    hello db 'Hello, World!',0

section .text
    global _start

_start:
    ; write the message to stdout
    mov eax, 4          ; sys_write system call
number
    mov ebx, 1          ; file descriptor 1 is stdout
    mov ecx, hello      ; address of the message
    mov edx, 13         ; length of the message
    int 0x80            ; make the system call

    ; exit the program
    mov eax, 1          ; sys_exit system call number
    xor ebx, ebx        ; exit code 0
    int 0x80            ; make the system call
```

This simple program makes use of the Linux system calls to write the string "Hello, World!" to the standard output and then exits.

**Step 3: Assembling and Running the Program** Once you've written the code, you need to assemble and link it using the following commands:

```bash
nasm -f elf32 hello.asm    # Assemble the code
ld -m elf_i386 -s -o hello hello.o  # Link the object
file
./hello  # Run the program
```

You should see the message "Hello, World!" printed to the screen.

## Conclusion

In this chapter, we've introduced you to the fundamentals of Assembly language, including its historical significance, its relationship with machine code, and its crucial role in modern computing. By understanding how Assembly works at the machine level, you've gained insight into how computers execute programs and how you can harness this knowledge to optimize your own code.

In the hands-on project, you wrote your first Assembly program, which is the first step in unlocking the power of low-level programming. In the next chapter, we'll dive deeper into the Assembly workflow, including how to use tools like assemblers, linkers, and loaders to bring your code to life.

By the end of this book, you'll be able to write high-performance, optimized Assembly code that interacts directly with the hardware, giving you the skills to tackle complex systems programming tasks. Let's get started!

# CHAPTER 2: THE ASSEMBLY LANGUAGE WORKFLOW

If you're new to the world of Assembly, it can seem like a far cry from the comfortable and abstracted world of high-level programming languages such as Python, Java, or C. While high-level languages are accessible and powerful, they are often too far removed from the hardware. In this chapter, we will explore how the language we write at a high level is translated down to something that a CPU can understand. We will also delve into the tools—assemblers, linkers, and loaders—that facilitate this process and learn about the structure of Assembly code.

By the end of this chapter, you will understand the flow of code from the high-level languages you know, such as Python, C, and Java, all the way down to Assembly language and machine code. This understanding will allow you to not only better appreciate the power of Assembly but also to create more efficient, optimized, and hardware-conscious programs.

## From High-Level Languages to Machine Code

Programming languages are designed to make human-computer interaction easier. But, at the lowest level, computers can only execute machine code—the binary instructions that directly manipulate the hardware. High-level languages like Python, C, and Java are abstracted ways to communicate with a computer, making it easier for humans to write software without worrying about hardware-specific details.

However, when you write code in one of these languages, the computer doesn't understand it directly. It needs to be translated into something the machine can execute. To make this happen, compilers and interpreters step in, converting your high-level code into an intermediate representation and eventually into machine code.

Let's break it down step by step:

1. **High-Level Language Code**: This is the code you write in C, Java, or Python. It's designed for ease of use and portability, which means you don't have to worry about the underlying machine architecture.
2. **Intermediate Representation**: In many cases, the high-level code first gets converted into an intermediate language. For example, Java code is compiled into bytecode, which runs on the Java Virtual Machine (JVM). While this allows Java programs to be portable, it's still not in the form the machine can directly execute.
3. **Compilation and Assembly**: In languages like C, the code gets compiled into Assembly or a lower-level language before being converted into machine code. This is where things start to get close to the hardware. The compiler turns your C code into Assembly, which is a series of mnemonics (human-readable representations of machine instructions) that the CPU can understand more easily.
4. **Machine Code**: Finally, the Assembly instructions are converted into binary machine code, which consists of 1s and 0s. The machine code tells the CPU exactly what operations to perform, how to move data around, and how to interact with the hardware.

# Translating C, Python, and Java into Assembly

Let's take a closer look at how different languages are translated into Assembly and machine code.

## C TO ASSEMBLY

C is one of the most commonly used low-level programming languages that gets directly compiled into Assembly. When you write a C program, a C compiler—like GCC—translates your high-level code into Assembly. Here's a simple example of a C program:

c

```
#include <stdio.h>

int main() {
    int x = 5;
    int y = 10;
    printf("The sum is: %d\n", x + y);
    return 0;
}
```

This program calculates the sum of two integers and prints it to the console. To see what happens behind the scenes, let's walk through the process of translating this C code into Assembly:

1.  **Preprocessing**: Before the C code is compiled, preprocessor directives like #include are processed. This includes the inclusion of libraries like stdio.h.
2.  **Compilation**: The C compiler reads the code and translates it into Assembly code, which is specific to the architecture of the CPU you're using. The code you wrote in C becomes a set of Assembly instructions.

3. **Assembly**: The Assembly code is then passed to the assembler, which converts it into machine code. The CPU doesn't understand the high-level concepts of variables and functions in C, but it does understand the Assembly instructions that correspond to those operations.

The result might look like this in Assembly:

```assembly
assembly

section .data
    fmt db 'The sum is: %d', 0

section .text
    global _start

_start:
    ; set x = 5
    mov eax, 5
    ; set y = 10
    mov ebx, 10
    ; calculate sum
    add eax, ebx
    ; print result
    push eax
    push fmt
    call printf
    ; exit program
    mov eax, 1
    xor ebx, ebx
    int 0x80
```

In this Assembly code, you can see the direct translation of the C instructions into the CPU's instructions, such as mov to move data between registers and add to perform arithmetic.

## PYTHON TO ASSEMBLY

Python, on the other hand, is an interpreted language, which means it doesn't compile directly to Assembly or machine code. Instead, Python code is executed by a Python interpreter. The interpreter reads the Python code and executes it step by step. However, Python programs can be compiled into bytecode, which is a lower-level representation that the Python interpreter can process.

While Python doesn't directly translate into Assembly, if you were to compile Python into machine code, it would follow a process similar to this:

1. **Source Code to Bytecode**: The Python interpreter takes your Python source code and compiles it into bytecode, an intermediate form that the interpreter can understand.
2. **Bytecode to Execution**: The Python interpreter then executes the bytecode. This execution involves translating Python's high-level operations into lower-level instructions, and eventually, machine code, via system calls and the underlying operating system.

The actual translation into Assembly is less direct in Python due to its interpreted nature. However, tools like Cython and PyInstaller can compile Python code to machine code for specific use cases.

## JAVA TO ASSEMBLY

Java works a bit differently. Instead of compiling directly to machine code or Assembly, Java code is compiled into an intermediate form called **bytecode**. This bytecode is platform-independent, which is why Java can run on different operating systems without needing to recompile the code.

1. **Source Code to Bytecode**: Java code is first compiled by the Java compiler (`javac`) into bytecode, which is a set of instructions designed to run on the Java Virtual Machine (JVM).
2. **JVM Execution**: The bytecode is then run by the JVM, which translates the bytecode into machine-specific code on the fly. The JVM is responsible for converting the bytecode into Assembly or machine code based on the underlying hardware architecture.
3. **JIT Compilation**: In some cases, the JVM uses Just-In-Time (JIT) compilation to convert bytecode into native machine code at runtime, further optimizing performance.

Though Java doesn't translate directly into Assembly, it's important to understand how this intermediate bytecode is ultimately converted into machine code and executed on hardware.

# Understanding Assemblers, Linkers, and Loaders

Now that we've seen how high-level languages get converted into Assembly and machine code, let's look at the tools that make this happen.

### ASSEMBLER

An assembler is a tool that converts Assembly code into machine code. The process of writing Assembly code involves using mnemonics—human-readable representations of machine instructions. These mnemonics are later translated into binary instructions that the CPU can execute directly.

For example, the `MOV` instruction in Assembly tells the CPU to move data into a register. The assembler takes this instruction and translates it into a binary code that the machine can understand.

Assemblers also perform other tasks, such as converting labels in Assembly code into memory addresses and handling macros (a set of instructions that are used repeatedly in a program).

## LINKER

Once an Assembly program is written and assembled into an object file (usually with a `.o` extension), it's not yet ready to run. To create a full executable program, you need a linker.

A linker's job is to combine object files into a single executable. It resolves references between object files, ensuring that functions and variables are correctly linked to their addresses in memory. The linker also adds necessary libraries to the executable.

For example, when you use a standard C library function like `printf`, the linker ensures that the program has access to the correct library and that the function call is properly mapped.

## LOADER

After the linker produces an executable file, it's still not ready to run directly. The loader is responsible for loading the executable into memory so that the CPU can begin executing it.

The loader places the program's instructions and data in appropriate memory locations. It also performs any necessary dynamic linking, where shared libraries are loaded into memory at runtime. Finally, it starts the program by transferring control to the first instruction in the executable.

## Analyzing Assembly Code: Structure and Syntax

Assembly code is structured in a very specific way. While each Assembly language is different (depending on the processor architecture), most share some basic elements.

1. **Mnemonics**: Mnemonics are short, human-readable representations of machine instructions. For example, MOV is used to move data between registers, and ADD is used for addition. These are the core elements of Assembly code.
2. **Operands**: Every Assembly instruction typically involves one or more operands. An operand is a value or reference that the instruction operates on. For example, in MOV AX, 5, AX is the destination operand (the register), and 5 is the source operand (the value to be moved).
3. **Labels**: Labels are used to mark positions in code that can be referenced by other instructions. They are commonly used in conjunction with branching instructions (e.g., JMP or CALL).

## Hands-On Project: Write an Assembly Program to Perform Simple Arithmetic Operations

Let's put everything we've learned into practice. In this hands-on project, we will write a simple Assembly program that performs basic arithmetic operations—addition, subtraction, multiplication, and division.

Here's the basic idea:

```assembly
assembly

section .data
    result db 'Result: %d', 0

section .text
    global _start

_start:
    ; Addition
    mov eax, 5
    mov ebx, 3
    add eax, ebx    ; eax = eax + ebx

    ; Subtraction
    mov ecx, 10
    sub ecx, 4      ; ecx = ecx - 4

    ; Multiplication
    mov edx, 6
    mov esi, 7
    mul edx         ; eax = eax * edx (multiplication
result)

    ; Division
    mov edi, 20
    mov ebx, 4
    div ebx         ; eax = eax / ebx (division
result)

    ; Exit
    mov eax, 1
    xor ebx, ebx
    int 0x80
```

In this example, we are using MOV to load values into registers, and then performing ADD, SUB, MUL, and DIV operations to manipulate the values in the registers. Finally, we use the int 0x80 system call to exit the program.

## Conclusion

In this chapter, we've explored how high-level languages like C, Python, and Java are translated into Assembly and ultimately machine code. We've also learned about the tools—assemblers, linkers, and loaders—that make this process possible. Understanding these workflows is crucial for becoming proficient in Assembly programming and optimizing code for performance.

The hands-on project gave you a glimpse of how these concepts work in practice, allowing you to write a basic Assembly program that performs arithmetic operations. With this knowledge in hand, you'll be well-prepared to dive deeper into the world of Assembly and low-level programming.

# CHAPTER 3: ASSEMBLY LANGUAGE FUNDAMENTALS

In this chapter, we will take a deep dive into the essential building blocks of Assembly language: mnemonics, registers, and the basic instruction set. These concepts form the core of any Assembly program, and understanding them is crucial to becoming proficient in low-level programming. We will also explore how control flow—especially conditional branching and loops—works in Assembly. By the end of this chapter, you'll be well-equipped to write more complex Assembly programs that interact with data, control program flow, and make decisions based on logic.

## Mnemonics and Registers

### WHAT ARE MNEMONICS AND HOW DO THEY RELATE TO MACHINE INSTRUCTIONS?

Assembly language is a low-level programming language that sits between high-level languages and machine code. It provides a more human-readable way to interact with the computer's hardware. But how do we bridge the gap between human-readable code and the binary machine instructions the CPU understands? The answer lies in **mnemonics**.

A mnemonic is a shorthand representation of a machine instruction. Rather than using raw binary or hexadecimal numbers to tell the CPU what to do, Assembly programmers use mnemonics—short, memorable words that represent complex operations. These mnemonics are then translated into machine code by an assembler, which the CPU can execute.

For example, consider the **MOV** instruction in Assembly. This mnemonic tells the CPU to "move" data from one location to another, typically between registers or between memory and a register. In machine code, the same operation might be represented by a binary number such as `0x8B`. But as you can see, **MOV** is much easier to remember and use than dealing with raw binary.

Here's an example of how mnemonics work in practice:

```assembly
MOV AX, 5    ; Move the value 5 into the AX register
```

In this case, the mnemonic `MOV` represents a machine instruction that tells the CPU to  the value 5 into the **AX** register. The value in the register can then be used for calculations or other operations. The assembler translates this instruction into machine code that the CPU understands.

Mnemonics are an abstraction that simplifies Assembly programming. Without mnemonics, we would need to write the raw binary codes for each instruction, which would be time-consuming and error-prone. By using mnemonics, programmers can focus on the logic of their programs without needing to memorize or work with low-level machine instructions directly.

## UNDERSTANDING REGISTERS AND THEIR ROLES IN ASSEMBLY PROGRAMMING

To understand how Assembly programming works, it's crucial to understand the **registers** in a CPU. A register is a small, fast storage location within the CPU that temporarily holds data that the processor is currently using. Registers are essential for almost every operation in Assembly programming. They serve as a bridge between the instructions the CPU executes and the memory where data is stored.

Registers are the most basic building blocks in Assembly language, and understanding how to use them effectively is key to writing efficient programs. Different registers have different roles, and each CPU architecture has its own set of registers.

Here are the most common types of registers:

1. **General-Purpose Registers (GPRs)**: These are used for a variety of tasks, including holding data for arithmetic operations, storing intermediate results, and acting as memory pointers. In x86 architecture, common general-purpose registers include **AX**, **BX**, **CX**, and **DX**. These registers can be accessed and modified by Assembly instructions.
2. **Segment Registers**: These registers are used in segmented memory models, where memory is divided into different sections. For example, the **CS** (Code Segment) register holds the starting address of the code segment, and the **DS** (Data Segment) register holds the starting address of the data segment. These registers help manage memory in certain architectures.
3. **Pointer and Index Registers**: These registers hold addresses used for accessing data in memory. For example, the **SP** (Stack Pointer) register points to the top of the stack,

and the **IP** (Instruction Pointer) register holds the address of the next instruction to be executed.

4. **Flags Register**: This register contains individual bits that represent the status of the processor. For example, the **ZF** (Zero Flag) is set if the result of an operation is zero, and the **CF** (Carry Flag) is set if an arithmetic operation generates a carry or borrow.

Let's take a closer look at how registers work in practice with an example. Consider the following Assembly code:

```assembly
MOV AX, 5    ; Store the value 5 in the AX register
MOV BX, 10   ; Store the value 10 in the BX register
ADD AX, BX   ; Add the value in BX to AX, result
stored in AX
```

In this example, the registers **AX** and **BX** hold the values 5 and 10, respectively. The `ADD` instruction adds the contents of **BX** to **AX**, storing the result (15) in **AX**. The registers act as temporary storage for the values involved in the operation, enabling the CPU to perform the addition quickly.

## Basic Instruction Set

Now that we understand the role of mnemonics and registers, let's turn our attention to the basic instruction set of Assembly language. These are the core operations that allow the CPU to manipulate data and control program flow.

## Arithmetic Instructions

Arithmetic instructions are used to perform mathematical operations on data. Some of the most common arithmetic instructions include:

- **MOV**: Moves data between registers or between memory and registers. This is not an arithmetic operation per se, but it is often used to set values before performing calculations.
- **ADD**: Adds the value of one operand to another. For example, `ADD AX, BX` adds the value in **BX** to **AX**.
- **SUB**: Subtracts the value of one operand from another. For example, `SUB AX, BX` subtracts the value in **BX** from **AX**.
- **MUL**: Multiplies two operands. In most Assembly languages, `MUL` is used for unsigned multiplication.
- **DIV**: Divides one operand by another. Like `MUL`, `DIV` typically operates on unsigned values.

These arithmetic instructions are the core tools for performing calculations in Assembly. They allow you to manipulate numbers directly in the CPU's registers, making them essential for everything from simple math to more complex algorithms.

## Logical Instructions

Logical instructions are used to perform bitwise operations on data. These are useful for tasks like setting or clearing specific bits in a value, comparing values, or performing boolean operations. Some of the most common logical instructions include:

- **AND**: Performs a bitwise AND operation between two operands. For example, `AND AX, BX` compares the bits in **AX** and **BX**, setting each bit in the result to 1 if both corresponding bits are 1.

- **OR**: Performs a bitwise OR operation. For example, `OR AX, BX` sets each bit in the result to 1 if at least one of the corresponding bits is 1.
- **XOR**: Performs a bitwise XOR (exclusive OR) operation. For example, `XOR AX, BX` sets each bit in the result to 1 if the corresponding bits in **AX** and **BX** are different.
- **NOT**: Performs a bitwise NOT operation, flipping all the bits in the operand. For example, `NOT AX` flips all the bits in **AX**.

Logical operations are essential for low-level programming, as they allow you to manipulate and test specific bits within a value. They are often used in tasks such as flag manipulation, data encoding, and optimization.

## DATA MOVEMENT INSTRUCTIONS

Data movement instructions are used to move data between registers, memory, and I/O ports. These instructions allow you to load, store, and transfer data within the system. Some of the most important data movement instructions include:

- **MOV**: Moves data from one location to another. For example, `MOV AX, 5` stores the value 5 in the **AX** register.
- **PUSH**: Pushes data onto the stack. The stack is a special region of memory used to store data temporarily, often during function calls.
- **POP**: Pops data off the stack. This instruction retrieves data that was previously pushed onto the stack.
- **IN**: Reads data from an I/O port into a register. This is typically used for interfacing with external devices.
- **OUT**: Sends data from a register to an I/O port. This is used to send data to external devices.

These instructions are the backbone of Assembly programming, allowing you to manipulate data in a way that's efficient and direct.

Data movement is crucial for most tasks in low-level programming, especially when dealing with hardware interfaces or optimizing memory usage.

# Control Flow

Control flow refers to the order in which instructions are executed in a program. In Assembly language, control flow is governed by **conditional branching** and **loops**, which allow a program to make decisions and repeat operations based on certain conditions.

### CONDITIONAL BRANCHING

Conditional branching is a fundamental part of programming, allowing a program to decide which path to take based on certain conditions. In Assembly, this is typically done using **jump** instructions.

- **JMP**: An unconditional jump to a specified label. For example, `JMP label` jumps to the location in the program marked by `label`.
- **JE (Jump if Equal)**: Jumps to a label if the zero flag (ZF) is set, meaning the result of a comparison was zero.
- **JNE (Jump if Not Equal)**: Jumps to a label if the zero flag is not set.
- **JC (Jump if Carry)**: Jumps if the carry flag is set, indicating that an arithmetic operation resulted in a carry.
- **JNC (Jump if No Carry)**: Jumps if the carry flag is not set.

These conditional jump instructions allow a program to make decisions based on the outcome of operations. For example, after performing a comparison (like checking if two values are equal), you can use a conditional jump to either take one path or another in the program.

Loops are essential for repetitive tasks. While high-level languages offer convenient loop constructs like `for` and `while`, in Assembly, you'll need to create loops manually using jump instructions and conditions.

For example, a simple loop that counts from 1 to 10 might look like this in Assembly:

```assembly

MOV CX, 1       ; Set CX to 1 (the counter)
MOV DX, 10      ; Set DX to 10 (the limit)

loop_start:
    ; Your code here (e.g., print CX)
    INC CX          ; Increment CX by 1
    CMP CX, DX      ; Compare CX with DX
    JL loop_start ; Jump to loop_start if CX is less
than DX
```

This loop will run until **CX** reaches 10, incrementing each time. The `CMP` instruction compares the value in **CX** with **DX**, and the `JL` (jump if less) instruction causes the loop to continue if the condition is true.

# Hands-On Project: Writing Assembly Code for Conditional Statements and Loops

Now that we've covered the basics of conditional branching and loops in Assembly, let's write a practical program that uses both concepts. In this project, we'll write an Assembly program that checks if a number is even or odd and prints a message accordingly. We'll also use a loop to count from 1 to 10.

```assembly
assembly

section .data
    even_msg db 'Even', 0
    odd_msg db 'Odd', 0

section .bss
    num resb 1

section .text
    global _start

_start:
    MOV AL, 5       ; Load the number to check (5 for odd)
    MOV BL, 2       ; Load the divisor (2 for even/odd check)

    ; Check if the number is even or odd
    DIV BL          ; Divide AL by 2 (result in AL, remainder in AH)
    CMP AH, 0       ; Compare remainder (AH) with 0
    JE even         ; Jump to 'even' if remainder is 0

    ; If odd
    MOV ECX, odd_msg
    JMP print

even:
    MOV ECX, even_msg

print:
    ; Print the result (simulating print here)
    ; Normally, you'd use a system call or library function to print
    ; For simplicity, this part is skipped in the code snippet

    ; Loop from 1 to 10
    MOV ECX, 1      ; Start the counter at 1
    MOV EDX, 10     ; Set loop limit to 10

loop_start:
    ; Print current counter (simulating print here)
```

```
    INC ECX             ; Increment the counter
    CMP ECX, EDX        ; Compare the counter with the
limit
    JL loop_start       ; Jump back to loop_start if
counter is less than 10

    ; Exit the program
    MOV EAX, 1
    XOR EBX, EBX
    INT 0x80            ; Exit
```

In this program, we use **DIV** to divide the number by 2 and check the remainder in **AH**. If the remainder is zero, the number is even; otherwise, it's odd. We also use a loop to count from 1 to 10, incrementing each time.

## Conclusion

In this chapter, we've covered some of the most fundamental aspects of Assembly programming: mnemonics, registers, basic instructions, and control flow. These concepts are essential for writing any kind of Assembly program, and mastering them will give you a deeper understanding of how programs interact with the CPU and memory.

We also explored how to write conditional statements and loops in Assembly, essential tools for writing complex programs. The hands-on project allowed you to put these concepts into practice, reinforcing your understanding of how Assembly handles data and control flow.

With these tools under your belt, you're now ready to start writing more complex Assembly programs that can interact with data, perform calculations, and control the flow of execution

# CHAPTER 4: OPTIMIZING CODE WITH ADVANCED ASSEMBLY TECHNIQUES

In previous chapters, we covered the fundamental elements of Assembly language: mnemonics, registers, instructions, and basic control flow. Now, we take the next step into more advanced topics: code optimization. When working with Assembly, one of the greatest advantages is the ability to fine-tune your programs to maximize performance. Whether it's reducing memory usage, improving processing speed, or finding the perfect balance between the two, optimizing Assembly code is a critical skill that can elevate your programming from functional to efficient.

This chapter will explore techniques for optimizing Assembly code, strategies for identifying and resolving bottlenecks, and how to balance speed and memory usage for optimal performance. We will also discuss the concept of **inline Assembly**—a method of integrating Assembly language into high-level languages like C. By the end of this chapter, you will have a deeper understanding of how to write high-performance Assembly code and when to leverage it for maximum efficiency.

## Code Optimization Strategies

Before diving into the technical aspects, it's important to understand the broader concept of code optimization in the context of Assembly. Optimization in Assembly programming refers to improving the performance of your code, often in terms of speed, memory usage, or both. In general, optimization should aim for

**cleaner, faster**, and **more efficient** code. Let's break down some of the most effective strategies for achieving that goal.

One of the first steps in optimizing any program is identifying where the bottlenecks are—the parts of your program that slow it down the most. Bottlenecks can exist in many forms, such as inefficient algorithms, excessive memory usage, or slow data transfers between registers and memory.

Here are some common sources of bottlenecks in Assembly programs:

1. **Slow Operations**: Some instructions are inherently slower than others, and using them excessively can slow down your program. For example, division is generally slower than addition or subtraction. Similarly, accessing memory (especially random memory access) can be much slower than manipulating data in registers.
2. **Inefficient Algorithms**: The choice of algorithm has a profound impact on performance. An algorithm with a high time complexity can significantly reduce the speed of your program, no matter how optimized the Assembly code is.
3. **Excessive Memory Usage**: Using too much memory, or inefficient memory access patterns, can slow down your program. For example, unnecessary memory allocations or poor memory layout can increase cache misses, leading to slower performance.

To identify these bottlenecks, a common technique is **profiling**. Profiling tools measure how much time the CPU spends on each part of your program. By using a profiler, you can pinpoint which sections of the code consume the most resources and focus your optimization efforts there.

## OPTIMIZING MEMORY USAGE

Memory optimization is one of the key areas where Assembly shines. Because Assembly language gives you direct control over the CPU's memory management, you can fine-tune how your program uses memory. Here are several ways to optimize memory usage:

1. **Use Registers Wisely**: Registers are the fastest type of memory in the CPU, so the more you can use them, the better. Minimizing the amount of time spent accessing slower types of memory (like RAM) can significantly improve performance.
2. **Optimize Data Access Patterns**: Memory access patterns can have a significant impact on performance, especially when dealing with large datasets. Accessing memory sequentially is much faster than accessing it randomly, because modern CPUs use cache memory to speed up sequential reads. Keeping your data structures contiguous and accessing them in order can improve cache utilization.
3. **Minimize Memory Allocations**: Excessive memory allocations can lead to fragmentation and increased memory usage. Try to allocate memory in large blocks and reuse it when possible, rather than frequently allocating and deallocating memory.
4. **Use Memory-Mapped I/O**: For applications that interact with hardware or perform heavy I/O operations, memory-mapped I/O allows you to read from and write to memory locations that correspond directly to hardware registers. This is an efficient way to handle I/O operations without the need for expensive function calls.

## SPEED VS. SIZE TRADE-OFFS

In optimization, there is often a trade-off between speed and size. A program that is highly optimized for speed may use more memory, while a program that is optimized for minimal memory usage might run slower. In Assembly programming, this is especially important, as you have to make conscious decisions about how to balance these two factors.

1. **Speed Optimization**: Speed optimization focuses on reducing the number of CPU cycles required to execute your code. This could involve using more registers, minimizing memory accesses, or using faster instructions. For example, if you need to perform a division, and you know that the divisor is a power of two, you can use a **shift** operation instead of a division, as shifting is much faster than division.
2. **Size Optimization**: On the other hand, size optimization focuses on reducing the memory footprint of your program. This can be important in embedded systems or other environments where memory is limited. You can achieve this by using fewer registers, reducing the size of data structures, or even using shorter instructions.

The challenge lies in balancing these two factors. For example, using more registers can make your code faster, but it can also use up more memory. Similarly, you might use complex optimizations to reduce memory usage, but they could slow your code down if they involve multiple memory accesses.

To strike the right balance, you need to consider the specific requirements of your program. If speed is the most critical factor (such as in real-time systems or games), then focusing on speed optimization might be your top priority. If you're working with a resource-constrained environment (like an embedded system with limited RAM), size optimization might take precedence.

## ADVANCED TECHNIQUES FOR OPTIMIZING ASSEMBLY CODE

Now that we have a good grasp of optimization strategies, let's explore some advanced techniques to make your Assembly code even more efficient.

1.  **Loop Unrolling**: Loop unrolling is a technique where the iterations of a loop are expanded into multiple operations, reducing the overhead of the loop control. This can improve performance by minimizing the number of jumps (branch instructions) the CPU has to make.

    For example, consider the following loop in Assembly:

    ```assembly
    MOV CX, 100      ; Loop 100 times
    loop_start:
        ADD AX, 1    ; Increment AX by 1
        DEC CX       ; Decrement counter
        JNZ loop_start ; Jump if CX is not zero
    ```

    This loop can be unrolled to something like this:

    ```assembly
    MOV CX, 50       ; Loop 50 times
    loop_unrolled:
        ADD AX, 2    ; Increment AX by 1 twice
        ADD AX, 2    ; Increment AX by 1 twice
        DEC CX       ; Decrement counter
        JNZ loop_unrolled
    ```

    By unrolling the loop, we reduce the number of jumps, which can improve performance in some situations.

2.  **Instruction Scheduling**: The order in which instructions are executed can have an impact on performance. CPUs have

pipelines that allow them to execute instructions concurrently, but some instructions may need to wait for others to complete. By carefully ordering your instructions, you can maximize the throughput of the CPU.

For example, if you have an operation that is dependent on the result of a previous one, you might introduce **no-op** (no-operation) instructions to allow the CPU to execute other instructions while waiting. This technique, known as **instruction pipelining**, can help make your code more efficient.

3. **Using SIMD Instructions**: SIMD (Single Instruction, Multiple Data) allows you to perform the same operation on multiple pieces of data at the same time. Many modern processors support SIMD instructions, such as Intel's **SSE** (Streaming SIMD Extensions) or **AVX** (Advanced Vector Extensions).

   By using SIMD, you can speed up operations like matrix multiplication or vector addition. For example, instead of performing multiple ADD instructions one by one on an array of values, you can use a single SIMD instruction to add multiple values simultaneously.

   ```
   assembly

   ; Example using SSE to add two arrays of
   numbers
   movaps xmm0, [array1]  ; Load first array into
   xmm0 register
   movaps xmm1, [array2]  ; Load second array into
   xmm1 register
   addps xmm0, xmm1       ; Add the arrays
   together in parallel
   movaps [result], xmm0  ; Store the result
   ```

SIMD can dramatically improve performance in data-intensive applications, especially in fields like image processing and scientific computing.

## 4. Inlining Assembly in C

Sometimes, you might want to mix the power of high-level programming with the performance of low-level Assembly. This is where **inline Assembly** comes in. Inlining Assembly allows you to embed Assembly instructions directly within your C code, giving you more control over performance without having to write an entire program in Assembly.

In C, inline Assembly is typically written using the `__asm` or `asm` keyword, depending on the compiler. Here's an example of how you might use inline Assembly to perform a quick optimization in a C program:

c

```c
#include <stdio.h>

int main() {
    int result;
    int a = 10, b = 5;

    // Inline Assembly to perform an optimized addition
    __asm__ (
        "addl %%ebx, %%eax;"
        : "=a"(result)    // Output to 'result'
        : "a"(a), "b"(b) // Inputs 'a' and 'b'
    );

    printf("The result is: %d\n", result);
    return 0;
}
```

In this example, the C code takes two variables `a` and `b`, and performs an addition operation directly using Assembly within the C code. This approach is particularly useful when you need to optimize specific sections of your program while still keeping the rest of the code in a high-level language.

# Hands-On Project: Implementing an Optimized Sorting Algorithm in Assembly

In this project, we will implement an optimized version of the **bubble sort** algorithm in Assembly. The goal is to improve its performance and make it as efficient as possible in terms of both speed and memory usage.

## STEP 1: BASIC BUBBLE SORT IMPLEMENTATION

The standard bubble sort algorithm works by repeatedly stepping through the list of elements, comparing adjacent items and swapping them if they are in the wrong order. The process repeats until the list is sorted.

Here's a simple implementation in Assembly:

```assembly
section .data
    arr db 5, 3, 8, 1, 2, 7 ; Array to be sorted
    arr_size db 6             ; Size of the array

section .text
    global _start

_start:
    MOV SI, 0                ; SI register is the outer
loop counter
```

```asm
    MOV DI, 1              ; DI register is the inner
loop counter
    MOV CX, [arr_size]  ; Load the array size

outer_loop:
    MOV BX, SI            ; Set BX to SI (outer loop
counter)
    MOV DX, [arr_size]  ; Load the array size into DX

inner_loop:
    MOV AL, [arr + BX]  ; Load the current element
into AL
    MOV AH, [arr + BX + 1]  ; Load the next element
into AH
    CMP AL, AH            ; Compare the two elements
    JG swap              ; Jump to swap if AL > AH

next_element:
    INC BX               ; Move to the next element
    DEC DI               ; Decrement the inner loop
counter
    JNZ inner_loop       ; Repeat inner loop if not
zero

outer_loop_continue:
    INC SI               ; Move to the next outer loop
    CMP SI, DX           ; Check if we've gone through
the whole array
    JL outer_loop        ; Continue outer loop if
necessary

swap:
    ; Swap the elements in AL and AH
    XCHG AL, AH          ; Swap the values
    MOV [arr + BX], AL  ; Store the swapped values
back into the array
    MOV [arr + BX + 1], AH

    ; Continue with the next element
    JMP next_element
```

## STEP 2: OPTIMIZATION CONSIDERATIONS

Although the basic bubble sort works, it is inherently inefficient. We can optimize it by:

1. **Eliminating Unnecessary Passes**: Once the largest elements are at the end of the array, they don't need to be checked again. We can adjust the loop to exclude the already sorted elements.
2. **Minimizing Memory Usage**: We can make sure to use registers efficiently and avoid unnecessary memory accesses.

## STEP 3: IMPLEMENTING THE OPTIMIZED ALGORITHM

We can implement the optimized bubble sort by stopping earlier if no swaps are made in a given pass, reducing unnecessary comparisons.

# Conclusion

In this chapter, we have covered several essential techniques for optimizing Assembly code. We explored strategies for identifying and resolving bottlenecks, optimizing memory usage, and balancing speed and size. We also delved into advanced techniques such as loop unrolling, instruction scheduling, SIMD, and inlining Assembly in C.

By understanding these optimization strategies and learning how to apply them, you can significantly improve the performance of your programs. Through the hands-on project, we saw how to implement a more efficient sorting algorithm in Assembly. With these tools in your toolbox, you are now ready to tackle more complex and performance-critical projects in Assembly programming.

# CHAPTER 5: MEMORY MANAGEMENT AND ADDRESSING

In any computing system, memory is one of the most crucial resources. From holding running programs to providing storage for data, how a program interacts with memory can have a significant impact on its performance. This chapter explores the ins and outs of memory management in Assembly programming, diving deep into how memory is organized, how it can be accessed, and the different methods used to manage it effectively.

By the end of this chapter, you will have a strong understanding of memory hierarchy, the various types of memory used by a CPU, addressing modes in Assembly, and the role of the stack and heap. Additionally, you will learn how to manage memory through practical hands-on projects, including writing a simple memory allocation program in Assembly.

## Memory Hierarchy and Access Methods

### DIFFERENT TYPES OF MEMORY AND THEIR ACCESS SPEEDS

Memory in a computer system is typically organized into a hierarchy based on speed and size. Each level of the memory hierarchy has a trade-off between its access speed and storage capacity. Understanding this hierarchy is crucial for optimizing your code, especially when writing Assembly programs that need to interact with hardware efficiently.

1. **Registers** Registers are the fastest form of memory in a CPU. They are small, temporary storage locations within the processor used to hold data that the CPU is currently processing. Registers are integral to almost all Assembly operations, as they provide the fastest access to data. When you write Assembly code, you will often use registers to perform calculations, move data around, and control program flow. The most common registers include **AX**, **BX**, **CX**, and **DX** in x86 architecture, though there are many other specialized registers for different tasks.

   Registers are crucial because they provide near-instantaneous access to data. However, because there are a limited number of registers, you must be strategic in how you use them. Mismanagement of registers can lead to performance issues, as the CPU will be forced to use slower memory for intermediate results.

2. **Cache** The next level of the memory hierarchy is **cache memory**. Cache is a small, but very fast, form of memory that sits between the CPU and the main memory (RAM). Cache is designed to store frequently accessed data to speed up operations. There are typically multiple levels of cache, with **L1** cache being the closest to the CPU and the fastest, followed by **L2** and **L3** caches.

   The main advantage of cache memory is its speed. However, it is much smaller than RAM, so it can only hold a limited amount of data. Caches are often used to store instructions and data that are repeatedly accessed, such as loop variables or frequently used functions.

3. **RAM (Random Access Memory)** **RAM** is the primary memory used by programs when they are running. It is much larger than cache memory but slower to access. RAM holds data and instructions that are actively used by running

programs. When your program is executing, it loads instructions and data from the hard disk or SSD into RAM, allowing the CPU to access them as needed.

The key feature of RAM is its ability to be accessed randomly, meaning any byte of memory can be accessed directly without needing to follow a sequence. However, because RAM is much slower than registers and cache, accessing data from RAM will inevitably introduce delays, especially if the memory accesses are not optimized.

4. **Hard Drive / SSD** Finally, storage devices such as hard drives (HDD) or solid-state drives (SSD) offer much larger storage capacities, but these are much slower than any form of RAM or cache. When data is not actively used by the program, it is stored in permanent memory like a hard drive or SSD. Accessing data from these devices is slow compared to RAM, cache, or registers.

   **SSD** technology is significantly faster than HDDs, but both still lag far behind the speed of in-memory data access.

The key takeaway here is that the faster the memory, the smaller the capacity. Registers provide the fastest access but are limited in number. RAM provides larger storage but slower access, and SSDs provide vast storage capacity at the cost of speed. As a programmer, understanding this hierarchy will allow you to make decisions about which types of memory to use and when, optimizing performance and efficiency in your programs.

## Access Methods

Each level of memory in the hierarchy uses different access methods. Let's break these down:

- **Direct Memory Access (DMA)**: A system where peripherals (like disk drives or network interfaces) can access memory directly, without involving the CPU. This speeds up data transfers for input/output (I/O) operations, freeing up the CPU for other tasks.
- **Memory-Mapped I/O**: In some systems, I/O devices (like graphics cards or network cards) are treated as memory locations. Memory-mapped I/O allows the CPU to read from and write to these devices using regular memory instructions, providing a streamlined way to interact with hardware.
- **Memory Caching**: This refers to the process of storing copies of frequently accessed data in a faster-access memory area (cache) to reduce the time it takes to retrieve that data. Caching improves the performance of data retrieval, especially when accessing large datasets or performing repetitive calculations.

## Addressing Modes in Assembly

One of the most important aspects of Assembly programming is the ability to access and manipulate data stored in memory. Assembly provides several types of **addressing modes** that define how an operand (a value or memory location) is accessed. Understanding these modes is essential for writing efficient Assembly code.

### IMMEDIATE ADDRESSING

Immediate addressing is the simplest form of addressing, where the operand is a constant value specified directly in the instruction itself. This mode is used when you want to work with constant values instead of memory locations.

For example:

```assembly
MOV AX, 5  ; Move the immediate value 5 into the AX
register
```

In this case, the value 5 is immediately available and does not need to be fetched from memory. This is the fastest form of addressing since there are no memory lookups involved.

## DIRECT ADDRESSING

In **direct addressing**, the operand is located at a specific memory address. The instruction specifies the address where the data is stored, and the CPU retrieves the data from that location.

For example:

```assembly
MOV AX, [0x1234]  ; Move the value from memory
address 0x1234 into the AX register
```

In this example, the value at memory address 0x1234 is moved into the **AX** register. Direct addressing is efficient because it directly specifies the memory location, but it requires that the data already exists at that location.

## INDIRECT ADDRESSING

Indirect addressing allows more flexibility by using a register or memory location to store the address of the operand. This means the address of the operand is not specified directly in the instruction but instead is retrieved from another register or memory location.

For example:

```
assembly
```

```
MOV BX, 0x1234        ; Load the address 0x1234 into BX
MOV AX, [BX]          ; Move the value at memory
address in BX (0x1234) into AX
```

In this case, the memory address 0x1234 is stored in the **BX** register, and the MOV instruction retrieves the data at that address. This form of addressing allows you to work with dynamically changing memory locations and is often used when working with arrays or pointers.

## INDEXED ADDRESSING

Indexed addressing is a method where a value is stored at a memory location determined by adding an offset to a base address stored in a register. This is commonly used when working with arrays or data structures.

For example:

```
assembly
```

```
MOV AX, [BX + 4]   ; Move the value at the address (BX
+ 4) into AX
```

In this example, **BX** contains the base address, and 4 is the offset. This type of addressing allows for efficient traversal of data structures like arrays, where each element is stored at a fixed distance (offset) from the previous element.

# Memory Mapping and Stack Management

## UNDERSTANDING THE STACK

In Assembly, the **stack** is a region of memory used to store data temporarily during program execution. It works on a **Last In, First Out (LIFO)** principle, where the most recently pushed data is the first to be popped off.

The stack is critical for managing function calls, as it stores return addresses and local variables. In Assembly, you manipulate the stack directly using **PUSH** and **POP** instructions:

```assembly
PUSH AX    ; Push the value in AX onto the stack
POP BX     ; Pop the value from the stack into BX
```

The **stack pointer (SP)** register keeps track of the current position in the stack, pointing to the last pushed item. When data is pushed onto the stack, the **SP** is decremented, and when data is popped off, the **SP** is incremented.

## THE HEAP

In addition to the stack, programs often use the **heap** for dynamic memory allocation. The heap is a region of memory used for variables whose size and lifetime are not known in advance. Unlike the stack, which is used for temporary data, the heap allows for **dynamic memory allocation** during the program's execution.

Heap memory is managed using functions like **malloc** in C, which allocate memory from the heap for use during the program's execution. While Assembly doesn't have built-in functions for heap management, it can interact with system calls or low-level memory allocation routines to allocate and free memory dynamically.

In Assembly, the **data section** is where initialized global or static variables are stored. These variables are given fixed memory addresses and are available for the entire duration of the program's execution. The data section is often used for storing constants or variables that are shared between different parts of the program.

# Hands-On Project: Creating a Simple Memory Allocation Program in Assembly

Now that we've covered the theory behind memory management and addressing, let's dive into a hands-on project where we will create a simple memory allocation program in Assembly.

### STEP 1: MEMORY ALLOCATION USING SYSTEM CALLS

In most operating systems, low-level memory allocation is managed using system calls. In Linux, for example, we can use the `brk` or `mmap` system calls to request memory from the operating system.

Here is a simple example using the `brk` system call to allocate memory dynamically:

```
assembly

section .data
    size db 256  ; Size of memory to allocate (256
bytes)

section .text
```

```
    global _start

_start:
    ; Get the current program break
    mov eax, 45             ; sys_brk system call
    xor ebx, ebx            ; Set EBX to 0 to get
current break
    int 0x80                ; Invoke system call

    ; Allocate memory by increasing the program break
    mov ebx, size           ; Load size into EBX
    add ebx, eax            ; Calculate new break
address
    mov eax, 45             ; sys_brk system call again
    int 0x80                ; Invoke system call

    ; Exit the program
    mov eax, 1              ; sys_exit system call
    xor ebx, ebx            ; Exit code 0
    int 0x80                ; Invoke system call
```

In this example, we first use the `sys_brk` system call to get the current program break (the end of the allocated memory). Then, we increase the program break by the amount of memory we want to allocate. This is a simple example of how memory can be allocated dynamically in Assembly using system calls.

## Conclusion

In this chapter, we've explored the crucial concepts of memory management and addressing in Assembly programming. We've learned about the different types of memory, from registers and cache to RAM and storage, and how each level of memory hierarchy affects performance. We also delved into various addressing modes, which define how data is accessed in Assembly.

We also took a closer look at the **stack**, **heap**, and **data sections**, understanding their role in managing memory during program execution. Finally, through a hands-on project, we implemented a simple memory allocation program in Assembly using system calls.

By mastering memory management and addressing in Assembly, you gain the power to write more efficient, optimized programs that interact directly with hardware.

# CHAPTER 6: THE ROLE OF OPTIMIZED MACHINE CODE

In the world of Assembly programming, the true power of performance lies in how you interact with the CPU. Assembly language allows you to communicate directly with the hardware, which means you have the ability to optimize code for maximum efficiency. But how exactly does Assembly influence CPU performance, and what does it take to make sure your code runs as quickly and smoothly as possible?

In this chapter, we will explore how low-level performance works, how Assembly can directly influence CPU operations, and the importance of instruction selection. We'll also break down the differences between Assembly and machine code, providing a deep dive into how the two interact. By the end of this chapter, you'll have a solid understanding of how to write high-performance code in Assembly, including practical skills to implement optimized string manipulation techniques.

## Understanding Low-Level Performance

### HOW ASSEMBLY DIRECTLY INFLUENCES CPU PERFORMANCE

At its core, Assembly language operates at the intersection of software and hardware. When you write Assembly code, you're telling the CPU how to perform tasks with the data stored in memory. But beyond the basic instructions, your choice of which instructions to use and how you structure your code can have a dramatic impact on performance.

The performance of any program ultimately depends on how efficiently the CPU can execute the instructions you've written. Assembly allows you to dictate exactly how this happens. Unlike high-level languages, where much of the code execution is abstracted away, Assembly lets you optimize every instruction to work as efficiently as possible for the hardware you are targeting.

One of the key aspects of optimizing Assembly code is understanding how the CPU executes instructions. When a program is running, the CPU follows a simple process:

1. **Fetching**: The CPU fetches the next instruction from memory.
2. **Decoding**: It decodes the instruction to determine what operation needs to be performed.
3. **Executing**: The CPU performs the operation, which may involve manipulating data, performing arithmetic, or moving values between registers and memory.
4. **Storing**: Finally, the CPU stores the result of the operation in a register or memory.

The performance bottleneck often lies in this cycle, particularly in how instructions are fetched, decoded, and executed. Optimizing Assembly code means ensuring that these cycles are as efficient as possible.

The most critical factor affecting performance is the **instruction pipeline**. Modern CPUs are designed with multiple execution units and pipeline stages that allow them to execute multiple instructions in parallel. However, certain instructions or sequences of instructions can disrupt this pipeline, leading to delays and performance degradation.

Optimizing Assembly involves making sure that your instructions make the most out of the CPU's execution units and minimize pipeline stalls. For instance, using simple arithmetic or logical operations that are executed in parallel can significantly boost performance compared to complex, multi-step instructions that delay the CPU's ability to execute other tasks.

## CACHE USAGE AND MEMORY ACCESS

The CPU doesn't only deal with instructions; it also needs to access data stored in memory. One of the most important factors in optimizing performance is understanding how the CPU interacts with memory. While registers are fast and caches are relatively quick, accessing RAM can be slow.

To maximize performance, your Assembly code needs to minimize memory access as much as possible, especially when accessing slower memory like RAM. This means:

1. **Storing data in registers**: Keeping data in registers is the fastest way to access it. Whenever possible, try to limit the number of times data has to be moved between registers and memory.
2. **Optimizing memory access patterns**: Accessing memory sequentially, rather than randomly, is faster due to the way modern CPUs cache data. This is important when working with arrays or data structures, where accessing contiguous blocks of data can increase cache hit rates and improve performance.

## PIPELINE OPTIMIZATION AND INSTRUCTION DEPENDENCIES

A key area to optimize is the way instructions are executed in relation to each other. Modern CPUs use pipelines to execute multiple instructions at once. However, these pipelines can be disrupted if instructions depend on one another.

Consider the following simple code:

```assembly
MOV AX, 5      ; Move 5 into AX
ADD AX, BX     ; Add the value in BX to AX
```

In this example, the ADD instruction depends on the value in **AX**. The CPU will have to wait for the MOV instruction to complete before it can execute the ADD instruction. If the instructions were rearranged, like this:

```assembly
MOV AX, 5      ; Move 5 into AX
MOV CX, 3      ; Move 3 into CX
ADD AX, BX     ; Add the value in BX to AX
```

The CPU can start preparing the second MOV instruction while still working on the first, potentially reducing the wait time. The goal is to minimize these **instruction dependencies** and allow the CPU to use its pipeline more effectively.

## Efficient Instruction Selection

### CHOOSING THE RIGHT INSTRUCTIONS FOR OPTIMAL EXECUTION

The instructions you choose in Assembly have a direct impact on the performance of your code. Certain instructions are faster than others, and some can disrupt the CPU's pipeline or cause it to stall.

Efficient instruction selection is critical when optimizing Assembly code.

For example, let's compare the following two sets of instructions:

**Set 1**:

```assembly
MOV AX, 5      ; Move 5 into AX
ADD AX, BX     ; Add BX to AX
```

**Set 2**:

```assembly
MOV AX, 5      ; Move 5 into AX
ADD AX, AX     ; Add AX to AX
```

In the first set, the ADD instruction involves adding a value from memory (the value in **BX**) to **AX**. This requires the CPU to load the value from **BX** into a temporary register before performing the operation. In contrast, the second set of instructions uses the value in **AX** itself, which eliminates the need to load data from memory, making it faster.

When writing Assembly code, you want to minimize memory accesses and use simple, fast instructions. Certain instructions, like **ADD**, **SUB**, **MUL**, and **DIV**, are commonly used in most programs. However, using an instruction like **DIV** (division) can slow down performance significantly because division is a relatively slow operation compared to addition or subtraction. In performance-critical sections of your code, it's often a good idea to avoid expensive instructions and look for alternatives.

For example, if you need to divide by a power of two, using a **SHIFT** operation is much faster:

assembly

```
SHL AX, 1     ; Shift AX left by 1 (equivalent to
multiplying by 2)
SHR AX, 1     ; Shift AX right by 1 (equivalent to
dividing by 2)
```

This simple change can drastically improve the performance of your program when division or multiplication by powers of two is required.

## USING SPECIALIZED CPU INSTRUCTIONS

Modern CPUs include a variety of specialized instructions that can speed up certain operations. For instance, many CPUs include **SIMD** (Single Instruction, Multiple Data) instructions, which allow a single instruction to perform operations on multiple pieces of data simultaneously. If your program performs a lot of repetitive tasks on large datasets, SIMD instructions can dramatically speed up execution.

Here's an example using **SSE** (Streaming SIMD Extensions) on Intel processors to add two arrays of numbers:

assembly

```
MOVAPS xmm0, [array1]   ; Load the first array into
register xmm0
MOVAPS xmm1, [array2]   ; Load the second array into
register xmm1
ADDPS xmm0, xmm1        ; Add the values in xmm1 to
xmm0 (element-wise)
MOVAPS [result], xmm0   ; Store the result back to
memory
```

In this example, the `ADDPS` instruction adds the corresponding elements of two arrays simultaneously, dramatically improving performance compared to iterating over the arrays one element at a time.

## Machine Code vs. Assembly: What's the Difference?

At first glance, **machine code** and **Assembly language** might seem like the same thing—they both ultimately tell the CPU what to do. However, there are significant differences between the two.

1. **Assembly Language**: Assembly is a human-readable form of machine code. It uses mnemonics (e.g., `MOV`, `ADD`, `JMP`) to represent machine instructions, which makes it easier for programmers to understand and write. Assembly also allows for more control over hardware and performance optimization.
2. **Machine Code**: Machine code consists of binary or hexadecimal instructions that the CPU can execute directly. It is the lowest-level code, and it's specific to the architecture of the CPU. For example, an instruction like `MOV` in Assembly is translated into machine code as a binary number like `0x89`.

While Assembly code is human-readable, machine code is not. It's the raw, executable instructions that the CPU understands. As a programmer, you rarely write in machine code directly; instead, you write in Assembly, and an assembler translates it into machine code.

The distinction between these two is important because it shows the relationship between high-level programming, Assembly, and the actual execution of code on the hardware. Assembly is a bridge between high-level languages and the raw, binary machine instructions that the CPU processes. Writing efficient Assembly ensures that your code translates into machine instructions that are fast and optimized.

# Hands-On Project: Implementing Optimized String Manipulation in Assembly

Let's put everything we've learned into practice by implementing a simple yet optimized string manipulation routine in Assembly. The task is to write a program that takes a string, reverses it, and prints the reversed string to the console.

### STEP 1: SETTING UP THE DATA

We will start by defining the string we want to manipulate. We'll store it in the data section of our Assembly code.

```assembly
section .data
    input_string db 'Hello, World!', 0    ; Input
string (null-terminated)
    output_string db 13 dup(0)            ; Output
buffer (space for 13 characters)
```

Here, we define the string "Hello, World!" and an empty buffer for the output. The null-terminator (0) at the end of the input string marks the end of the string.

### STEP 2: REVERSING THE STRING

The next step is to reverse the string. To do this, we'll need to loop through the string, swapping the first and last characters, the

second and second-to-last characters, and so on. Here's the
Assembly code for this step:

```assembly
section .text
    global _start

_start:
    ; Initialize pointers
    mov esi, input_string       ; ESI points to the
beginning of the input string
    mov edi, output_string      ; EDI points to the
beginning of the output string

    ; Find the length of the string
    find_length:
        cmp byte [esi], 0       ; Check if we've
reached the null terminator
        je reverse_string       ; If yes, jump to
reverse_string
        inc esi                 ; Otherwise, move to
the next character
        jmp find_length

    reverse_string:
        ; Now reverse the string
        dec esi                        ; Move ESI to the
last character of the input string
        reverse_loop:
            mov al, [esi]       ; Load the character
into AL
            mov [edi], al       ; Store it in the
output string
            inc edi             ; Move the output
pointer forward
            dec esi             ; Move the input
pointer backward
            cmp esi, input_string ; Check if we've
reached the beginning
            jge reverse_loop    ; If not, continue
the loop
        ; Null-terminate the reversed string
```

```
mov byte [edi], 0
```

This program starts by finding the length of the string (by looking for the null terminator) and then reverses it in place. The result is stored in the `output_string` buffer.

STEP 3: DISPLAYING THE OUTPUT

Finally, we need to print the reversed string to the console. This can be done using a system call (on Linux):

```assembly
    ; Write the output string to stdout
    mov eax, 4          ; sys_write system call
    mov ebx, 1          ; File descriptor 1 (stdout)
    mov ecx, output_string ; Address of the reversed
string
    mov edx, 13         ; Length of the string
    int 0x80            ; Call the kernel
```

This code uses the `sys_write` system call to output the reversed string to the console.

# Conclusion

In this chapter, we've explored the role of optimized machine code in improving CPU performance. We learned how Assembly directly influences how efficiently the CPU can execute instructions, from the basics of the CPU's execution pipeline to more advanced techniques like instruction selection and SIMD instructions. We also examined the difference between Assembly and machine code and how they work together to execute programs on the CPU.

Through the hands-on project, you learned how to optimize a string manipulation routine in Assembly, improving performance by minimizing memory access and leveraging efficient instructions. With this knowledge, you are now equipped to write faster, more efficient programs in Assembly, tapping into the full power of the CPU for optimal performance.

# CHAPTER 7: DEBUGGING AND TROUBLESHOOTING ASSEMBLY CODE

When working with Assembly code, you're operating at the lowest level of software programming. This proximity to the hardware gives you unprecedented control over the CPU, memory, and the flow of instructions, but it also means that errors can be harder to spot and resolve. Unlike high-level languages where modern IDEs and compilers catch many types of errors, debugging Assembly requires a more hands-on, in-depth approach. This chapter will guide you through the process of debugging and troubleshooting Assembly code, covering common issues, the tools available for debugging, and manual debugging strategies.

By the end of this chapter, you'll be comfortable identifying and fixing issues in your Assembly programs using both automatic and manual debugging techniques. You will also gain hands-on experience with debugging a simple Assembly program, allowing you to put these techniques into practice.

## Common Issues in Assembly Code

### SEGMENTATION FAULTS

A **segmentation fault**, commonly known as a **segfault**, occurs when a program attempts to access a memory location that it's not allowed to access. This usually happens when there is an issue with memory addressing, such as when you attempt to read from or write to an invalid memory location. Segmentation faults are one of the most common errors in Assembly programming, and they can be challenging to debug due to the low-level nature of Assembly code.

### *What Causes Segmentation Faults?*

In Assembly, segmentation faults typically occur due to the following reasons:

1. **Dereferencing Null or Invalid Pointers**: If you try to access memory using an invalid address, the CPU will trigger a segmentation fault. This is often the result of incorrectly setting a pointer or attempting to access memory before it's been allocated.
2. **Stack Corruption**: Stack corruption is another common cause of segmentation faults. If you inadvertently overwrite the return address or local variables on the stack, it can cause the program to jump to an invalid location or use invalid data, leading to a segfault.
3. **Buffer Overflow**: A buffer overflow occurs when data is written beyond the allocated memory buffer. This can overwrite other variables or important control structures, causing the program to crash.

### *How to Prevent Segmentation Faults*

Preventing segmentation faults in Assembly code requires careful management of memory addresses and pointers. Always ensure that the pointers you're using to access memory are valid and that you're not accessing memory beyond the bounds of an allocated region. Additionally, use techniques such as bounds checking when dealing with arrays or buffers to prevent buffer overflows.

# Stack Overflow

A **stack overflow** occurs when the stack grows beyond its allocated memory limit. This is often caused by a recursive function or an excessive number of function calls. The stack is a special region of memory used to store function parameters, return addresses, and local variables. If too much data is pushed onto the stack, it can overflow, causing the program to crash.

## *What Causes Stack Overflows?*

1. **Deep Recursion**: Recursion is a common cause of stack overflows. Each recursive call pushes data onto the stack, and if the recursion goes too deep, the stack can overflow.
2. **Large Local Variables**: If a function declares large local variables or arrays, these can consume a significant amount of stack space. When this happens repeatedly, it can cause a stack overflow.
3. **Incorrect Stack Management**: If you manually push or pop values from the stack incorrectly, it can lead to stack corruption and eventual overflow.

## *How to Prevent Stack Overflows*

To avoid stack overflows, be mindful of the depth of recursion in your code. If your function calls are recursive, consider using an iterative solution instead. Additionally, ensure that your local variables are kept small, and if you need to allocate large amounts of memory, consider using the heap instead of the stack.

In Assembly, registers are your primary tool for storing and manipulating data. However, using them incorrectly can lead to errors in your program. Common issues with registers include:

1. **Overwriting Registers**: Registers are temporary storage locations, so overwriting a register that contains important data can cause unintended side effects. For example, if you overwrite a register that holds the result of an important calculation, you may lose that result without realizing it.
2. **Incorrect Register Usage**: Each register has a specific purpose or role in Assembly code. For instance, in the x86 architecture, **EAX** is commonly used for return values, **EBX** for base pointers, and **ECX** for counters. Using the wrong register for a specific task can lead to errors or inefficiencies.

### How to Prevent Register Misuse

Always be mindful of which registers you are using and their intended purposes. Make sure to back up important values in registers before overwriting them, especially when dealing with function calls or complex calculations. Additionally, use comments to document the role of each register in your program, as this can help prevent confusion later on.

# Using Debuggers and Profilers

## INTRODUCTION TO GDB (GNU DEBUGGER)

The **GNU Debugger (GDB)** is one of the most widely used tools for debugging Assembly and C programs. GDB allows you to run a program step by step, inspect variables, and set breakpoints to halt execution at specific points. It can be extremely helpful when debugging Assembly code, as it allows you to inspect the state of registers, memory, and the stack while the program is running.

## Basic GDB Commands

1. **gdb <program_name>**: Launch GDB and load the program to debug.
2. **break <function_name>**: Set a breakpoint at the beginning of a function.
3. **break <line_number>**: Set a breakpoint at a specific line of the program.
4. **run**: Start executing the program within GDB.
5. **step**: Execute the program one instruction at a time, stepping into function calls.
6. **next**: Execute the program one instruction at a time, stepping over function calls.
7. **print <variable_name>**: Print the value of a variable or register.
8. **info registers**: Display the current values of all CPU registers.
9. **continue**: Resume execution after hitting a breakpoint.

## Using GDB for Assembly Debugging

When debugging Assembly code with GDB, you can set breakpoints at specific memory locations or instructions to halt execution and inspect the state of your program. For example, if you suspect an issue with a specific register, you can use the `info registers` command to check its value at different points during execution.

## OTHER DEBUGGING TOOLS

While GDB is one of the most powerful debugging tools, there are other tools that can help you with debugging Assembly code:

1. **Valgrind**: A tool used to detect memory-related errors, such as memory leaks or invalid memory accesses. Valgrind is especially useful when debugging programs that interact heavily with memory.
2. **LLDB**: The debugger for the LLVM project. Similar to GDB, LLDB is used for debugging programs written in C, C++, and Assembly.
3. **Perf**: A performance analysis tool that helps you profile your program's execution, helping you identify performance bottlenecks.

## Manual Debugging Strategies

While debuggers like GDB are incredibly powerful, sometimes the best way to debug Assembly code is through a more manual approach. Here are some key manual debugging strategies:

### CHECKING MEMORY ADDRESSES

When debugging Assembly code, one of the first things you should do is verify that memory addresses are being accessed correctly. If you encounter a segmentation fault or memory corruption, it's important to check the memory addresses you're using to ensure they are valid.

To check memory addresses manually, you can:

1. **Print memory values**: In GDB, you can use the `x` (examine memory) command to print the contents of a specific memory address. For example, `x/4xb 0x1234` will print 4 bytes starting at memory address `0x1234` in hexadecimal.
2. **Inspect memory at different points**: To identify when memory gets corrupted or incorrectly modified, you can

check the memory before and after specific instructions execute.

3. **Verify stack integrity**: The stack is a common source of memory-related issues. You can manually check the values on the stack to ensure they are as expected, especially after function calls or when using **PUSH** and **POP** operations.

## CHECKING REGISTER VALUES

Another crucial part of debugging Assembly is checking the values stored in CPU registers. Mismanaging registers is a common cause of errors, especially when performing arithmetic operations or manipulating pointers. GDB provides several ways to inspect the contents of registers, which can help you pinpoint issues.

You can use the `info registers` command in GDB to view the current state of all registers, or you can print individual registers using the `print` command.

It's also helpful to track register values at various points during execution. For example, you may want to inspect a register before and after a calculation to verify that the operation has been performed correctly.

## INSTRUCTION FLOW

One of the most effective ways to debug Assembly code is to step through the instructions manually. This allows you to observe how each instruction affects the program state and track down the source of any issues.

Using GDB's `step` and `next` commands, you can execute the program one instruction at a time. This is especially useful for understanding the flow of control through your program and verifying that the correct instructions are being executed at the right time.

You can also use **tracepoints** in GDB to automatically record the sequence of instructions executed, which can be helpful for identifying where things go wrong in complex programs.

# Hands-On Project: Debugging a Simple Assembly Program with a Known Error

In this project, we will write a simple Assembly program with a known error and use debugging techniques to identify and fix the issue.

## STEP 1: WRITE THE PROGRAM

Here's the simple program:

```
assembly

section .data
    num1 db 5
    num2 db 10
    result db 0

section .text
    global _start

_start:
    MOV AL, [num1]      ; Load num1 into AL
    ADD AL, [num2]      ; Add num2 to AL
    MOV [result], AL    ; Store result in memory

    ; Exit program
    MOV EAX, 1          ; sys_exit system call
    XOR EBX, EBX        ; Exit code 0
    INT 0x80            ; Invoke system call
```

This program is supposed to add two numbers and store the result. However, it has a bug. Can you find it?

## STEP 2: DEBUGGING WITH GDB

Let's use GDB to debug this program.

1. **Set Breakpoints**: We'll set breakpoints at key locations in the program to inspect the state of registers and memory. Start by setting a breakpoint at the beginning of the program:

   bash

   ```
   gdb ./program
   (gdb) break _start
   ```

2. **Step Through the Program**: Step through the program line by line to observe the execution and check the contents of the registers:

   bash

   ```
   (gdb) run
   (gdb) step
   (gdb) info registers
   (gdb) print $al
   ```

3. **Check Memory**: Check the values in memory at each step to ensure that the numbers are being loaded and manipulated correctly:

   bash

   ```
   (gdb) x/1xb num1
   (gdb) x/1xb num2
   (gdb) x/1xb result
   ```

Upon debugging, we discover that the issue arises because **AL** is a byte register, but we are using it to perform arithmetic on 8-bit values. When the result exceeds 255, it wraps around, causing incorrect behavior.

The fix is to use a **word** register, like **AX**, which can hold 16-bit values.

```assembly
section .data
    num1 db 5
    num2 db 10
    result db 0

section .text
    global _start

_start:
    MOV AL, [num1]      ; Load num1 into AL
    ADD AL, [num2]      ; Add num2 to AL
    MOV [result], AL    ; Store result in memory

    ; Exit program
    MOV EAX, 1          ; sys_exit system call
    XOR EBX, EBX        ; Exit code 0
    INT 0x80            ; Invoke system call
```

## Conclusion

Debugging Assembly code requires a deep understanding of how the CPU interacts with memory, registers, and instructions. In this chapter, we've explored common issues like segmentation faults, stack overflows, and register misuse, and learned how to diagnose and resolve them using GDB and manual debugging techniques. By carefully inspecting memory addresses, register values, and instruction flow, you can identify and fix errors in your Assembly code with precision.

The hands-on project provided an opportunity to apply these debugging techniques in practice, reinforcing your ability to troubleshoot common issues and improve the quality of your Assembly programs. As you continue to write more complex programs, these debugging skills will be invaluable for ensuring your code runs efficiently and correctly.

# CHAPTER 8: USING ADVANCED ASSEMBLER TOOLS AND IDES

Writing Assembly code brings us to the very core of how computers work. It allows us to communicate directly with the hardware, giving us control over the CPU, memory, and even how we access data. However, writing Assembly by hand can be challenging. The language itself is cryptic and lacks the modern conveniences we often take for granted, such as automated memory management or high-level abstractions. To make our work easier and more productive, we rely on a variety of **tools and Integrated Development Environments (IDEs)** that assist us in writing, debugging, and optimizing Assembly programs.

In this chapter, we will explore some of the most popular **Assembly IDEs** and **assemblers**, such as **NASM** (Netwide Assembler), **MASM** (Microsoft Macro Assembler), and other tools. We will discuss the step-by-step process of **assembling, linking, and compiling** Assembly code into an executable file. Additionally, we will look at ways to automate repetitive tasks in Assembly programming using **scripts**. Finally, we'll guide you through a hands-on project where you'll set up your own Assembly development environment and create your first project.

## Assembly IDEs and Editors

An **IDE (Integrated Development Environment)** is a software suite that provides developers with the tools they need to write, test, and debug their code. In the case of Assembly programming, an IDE can provide syntax highlighting, debugging tools, and integration with assembler and linker utilities. There are several options for Assembly IDEs and text editors, each with its unique strengths.

## NASM (Netwide Assembler)

**NASM** is one of the most popular open-source assemblers available for x86 and x86-64 architectures. It is known for its ease of use, support for modern processors, and ability to generate highly optimized machine code. NASM is widely used for writing low-level code, especially in Linux-based environments.

### *Key Features of NASM:*

1. **Cross-Platform Compatibility**: NASM works on multiple platforms, including Linux, Windows, and macOS.
2. **Support for Multiple Output Formats**: NASM can produce object files, executables, and other types of machine code output.
3. **Flexibility in Syntax**: NASM allows users to write in a more readable, consistent syntax, making it accessible for both beginners and experienced developers.
4. **Optimization Features**: NASM can generate highly optimized code that is tailored for specific processors, giving users more control over performance.

### *Example of Using NASM:*

Here's a simple example of how you would use NASM to write and compile an Assembly program.

1. Write your Assembly code (e.g., `hello.asm`).
2. Assemble the code using NASM:

```bash
bash
```

```
nasm -f elf64 hello.asm
```

3. Link the object file to create an executable:

```bash
```

```
ld -s -o hello hello.o
```

4. Run the program:

```bash
```

```
./hello
```

## MASM (MICROSOFT MACRO ASSEMBLER)

**MASM** is the assembler that comes with Microsoft Visual Studio and is the most widely used assembler for Windows development. MASM supports both x86 and x64 assembly programming and provides a rich set of features for integrating assembly code into Windows applications.

### *Key Features of MASM:*

1. **Rich Integration with Windows**: MASM integrates well with the Windows operating system, allowing you to write system-level code and create Windows applications.
2. **Powerful Macros**: MASM supports macros, allowing you to create reusable code patterns and simplify complex tasks.
3. **Advanced Debugging Tools**: MASM comes with powerful debugging tools for Windows, such as the **Microsoft Debugger**.
4. **Object-Oriented Assembly**: MASM supports higher-level programming constructs such as structures and object-oriented programming, providing more abstraction.

### *Example of Using MASM:*

MASM is usually integrated with Visual Studio, but you can also use it via the **Command Prompt**:

1. Write your Assembly code (e.g., `hello.asm`).
2. Assemble the code using MASM:

   ```bash
   ml /c /coff hello.asm
   ```

3. Link the object file to create an executable:

   ```bash
   link hello.obj
   ```

4. Run the program:

   ```bash
   hello.exe
   ```

## IDES FOR ASSEMBLY PROGRAMMING

While NASM and MASM provide essential tools for Assembly programming, an IDE can greatly enhance your productivity by offering features like syntax highlighting, code completion, and debugging support.

1. **Visual Studio Code**: This free, open-source editor provides excellent support for many programming languages, including Assembly. With the right extensions, you can enable syntax highlighting, code snippets, and even debugging for Assembly code.

2. **Emacs**: Emacs is a highly customizable, text-based editor that also supports Assembly language through its various extensions and modes. It's particularly popular for those who prefer working with keyboard-centric tools.
3. **Sublime Text**: Sublime Text is another highly popular text editor known for its speed and simplicity. It supports Assembly programming through packages like "x86-64 Assembly" that add syntax highlighting and other tools.
4. **IDEAL (Integrated Development Environment for Assembly Language)**: Ideal is a powerful and specialized IDE specifically designed for Assembly programming. It includes a built-in debugger, assembly syntax checking, and an interactive interface.

### CHOOSING THE RIGHT ASSEMBLY EDITOR

Choosing the right IDE or editor depends largely on your needs and personal preferences. For simple projects, lightweight text editors like **Visual Studio Code** or **Sublime Text** might be sufficient, especially when combined with an external debugger like GDB. However, for more complex applications, MASM and Visual Studio provide a rich development environment tailored for Windows.

## Linking, Compiling, and Assembling Code

To bring your Assembly program to life, you need to follow a clear process involving **assembling**, **linking**, and **compiling**. This process transforms your human-readable Assembly code into machine code that the CPU can execute.

## ASSEMBLING THE CODE

The first step in turning your Assembly code into an executable is to assemble it. The **assembler** takes the human-readable Assembly code and translates it into **object code** (machine-readable binary code), which consists of machine instructions.

For example, with NASM, you can assemble your code like this:

```bash
nasm -f elf64 myprogram.asm
```

This command tells NASM to assemble the `myprogram.asm` file into an object file in **ELF64** format, which is a common format used in Linux systems. The output file will be a `.o` file (e.g., `myprogram.o`).

## LINKING THE OBJECT FILE

Once the Assembly code has been assembled into object code, it needs to be linked to form a complete executable. The **linker** combines object files and libraries into a single executable file. It also resolves references between different pieces of code.

For example, with **LD (Linux Linker)**, you can link an object file like this:

```bash
ld -s -o myprogram myprogram.o
```

The `-s` option strips unnecessary symbols from the final executable, and `-o myprogram` specifies the name of the output file.

For **MASM**, the linking process can be done using the **Linker**:

```bash
bash
```

```bash
link myprogram.obj
```

This links the object file into an executable.

## COMPILING (OPTIONAL STEP)

In some cases, especially when using higher-level Assembly or mixed-language programs, you may also need to compile your Assembly code. **Compilation** typically refers to the process of converting a high-level language (like C or C++) into Assembly code, which is then assembled and linked.

When writing pure Assembly, compilation is not strictly necessary, as the assembler handles the translation from Assembly to machine code directly. However, if your program involves calling C functions or using system libraries, you may need a **compiler** to prepare the code before assembling it.

For example, in a project involving both C and Assembly, you might use GCC to compile the C code and NASM to assemble the Assembly code:

```bash
bash
```

```bash
gcc -c mycode.c
nasm -f elf64 myprogram.asm
ld -o myprogram mycode.o myprogram.o
```

## CREATING AN EXECUTABLE

Once the code is assembled and linked, the result is an executable file. This file contains machine code that the operating system can run directly. The executable is typically a `.exe` file on Windows or a binary file on Linux/macOS.

# Automating Assembly Programming with Scripts

One of the challenges in Assembly programming is the repetitive nature of the work. You often need to assemble, link, and test your code multiple times, making the development process tedious. Fortunately, you can automate many of these steps using **scripts**.

### WRITING SHELL SCRIPTS FOR ASSEMBLY

On Linux and macOS, you can use **Bash** (the shell) to write scripts that automate the assembly and linking process. A typical script might look like this:

```bash
#!/bin/bash
# Assemble and link Assembly code

# Assemble the code with NASM
nasm -f elf64 myprogram.asm -o myprogram.o

# Link the object file to create the executable
ld -s -o myprogram myprogram.o

# Run the program
./myprogram
```

This script automates the process of assembling the code, linking the object file, and running the executable, saving you time during development.

## BATCH SCRIPTS FOR WINDOWS

On Windows, you can write **batch scripts** to automate the building of Assembly programs. Here's an example of a simple batch script for MASM:

```batch
@echo off
:: Assemble the code with MASM
ml /c /coff myprogram.asm

:: Link the object file
link myprogram.obj

:: Run the program
myprogram.exe
```

This script performs the same steps as the Bash script but is tailored for Windows using **MASM** and the **Linker**.

## USING MAKEFILES

If you're working on a larger project with multiple files, you can use a **Makefile** to automate the build process. A Makefile is a configuration file used by the **make** utility to compile and link programs automatically. Here's an example of a simple Makefile for Assembly:

```makefile
ASM = nasm
LD = ld
CFLAGS = -f elf64

all: myprogram

myprogram: myprogram.o
```

```
    $(LD) -s -o myprogram myprogram.o

myprogram.o: myprogram.asm
    $(ASM) $(CFLAGS) myprogram.asm -o myprogram.o

clean:
    rm -f *.o myprogram
```

In this Makefile:

- `make` will assemble and link the program.
- `make clean` will remove the object files and executable.

# Hands-On Project: Set Up a Development Environment for Assembly Programming and Build Your First Project

Now that we've covered the tools, IDEs, and scripts you can use for Assembly programming, let's walk through a hands-on project where you'll set up your own development environment and create your first Assembly project.

## STEP 1: INSTALL THE NECESSARY TOOLS

1. **For Linux/macOS**:
   o   Install NASM using the package manager:

   ```bash
   sudo apt install nasm    # For Ubuntu
   brew install nasm        # For macOS
   ```

   o   Install the **GCC** package for linking:

   ```bash
   ```

```
sudo apt install build-essential    # For
Ubuntu
brew install gcc                     # For
macOS
```

2. **For Windows**:
   - o    Install **MASM** through Visual Studio or use the
        **Windows SDK** for assembly programming.


## STEP 2: WRITE YOUR FIRST ASSEMBLY PROGRAM

Let's create a simple "Hello, World!" program in Assembly. Here's
the code:

```assembly
assembly

section .data
    hello db 'Hello, World!', 0

section .text
    global _start

_start:
    ; Write to stdout
    mov eax, 4          ; sys_write system call
    mov ebx, 1          ; file descriptor 1 is stdout
    mov ecx, hello      ; address of the string
    mov edx, 13         ; length of the string
    int 0x80            ; make the system call

    ; Exit the program
    mov eax, 1          ; sys_exit system call
    xor ebx, ebx        ; exit code 0
    int 0x80            ; make the system call
```

Save the program as `hello.asm`.

## Step 3: Assemble, Link, and Run the Program

Now that you have written your code, assemble, link, and run the program using the following commands:

```bash
nasm -f elf64 hello.asm -o hello.o
ld -s -o hello hello.o
./hello
```

This should display `Hello, World!` on the screen.

## Step 4: Automate the Build Process with a Script

Create a shell script to automate the assembly, linking, and execution process. Save the following as `build.sh`:

```bash
#!/bin/bash
nasm -f elf64 hello.asm -o hello.o
ld -s -o hello hello.o
./hello
```

Now, you can simply run `./build.sh` to automate the build process.

# Conclusion

In this chapter, we've covered the essential tools and techniques for Assembly programming. We explored different **Assembly IDEs** and editors, including **NASM** and **MASM**, and learned how to assemble and link code into an executable. Additionally, we examined how to automate repetitive tasks using **scripts** and **Makefiles** to streamline the development process.

Through the hands-on project, you set up your own development environment, wrote your first Assembly program, and automated the build process. With these tools and techniques at your disposal, you're now ready to take your Assembly programming to the next level, creating more complex projects and optimizing your workflow for greater efficiency.

# CHAPTER 9: REAL-WORLD APPLICATIONS OF ASSEMBLY LANGUAGE

Assembly language may seem like a relic from the past, but it still plays a critical role in modern computing. While high-level languages like Python, Java, and C dominate application development, Assembly remains indispensable in specific contexts that require low-level hardware interaction, performance optimization, and a deep understanding of system architecture. In this chapter, we will explore some of the most important real-world applications of Assembly language, focusing on embedded systems, operating system kernel development, and reverse engineering. We will also walk through a hands-on project where you'll build a simple program for an embedded system.

By the end of this chapter, you will have a deeper understanding of how Assembly continues to shape the world of computing, and you'll have gained practical experience in writing low-level code for embedded systems.

## Embedded Systems and Firmware Programming

### THE IMPORTANCE OF ASSEMBLY IN MICROCONTROLLERS AND EMBEDDED DEVICES

Embedded systems are specialized computing devices that often perform specific, critical tasks. These systems are used in everything from household appliances and automobiles to medical devices and industrial machines. Unlike traditional computers, embedded systems often have limited resources in terms of memory, processing power, and storage. This makes them ideal candidates for **Assembly language**, which allows developers to write highly efficient code that directly interacts with the hardware.

At the heart of many embedded systems are **microcontrollers**— small, low-power processors that control the device's operations. Microcontrollers typically feature a CPU, memory, and input/output (I/O) capabilities, all integrated into a single chip. Because of their constrained resources, optimizing microcontroller code for both speed and memory usage is essential, and this is where Assembly language shines.

Assembly gives developers precise control over how data is stored and accessed, and it allows them to fine-tune performance to the maximum. Whether it's an industrial control system, a drone, or a fitness tracker, embedded systems rely on code that is lean and fast. In such cases, using a high-level language could introduce inefficiencies that lead to performance bottlenecks or memory overruns, which are unacceptable in embedded environments. By writing in Assembly, developers can ensure their code is as efficient as possible, taking full advantage of the available hardware.

## MICROCONTROLLER PROGRAMMING IN ASSEMBLY

When working with microcontrollers, one of the first things you'll do is interact directly with the hardware. This involves using **peripherals**, such as timers, sensors, and communication interfaces (e.g., UART, SPI, I2C). Assembly is particularly useful in this context because it allows you to write code that interfaces directly with these peripherals without relying on high-level abstraction layers.

Consider the task of turning on an LED connected to a microcontroller. In a high-level language like C, this would involve using a library to interface with the hardware. In Assembly, however, you interact directly with the microcontroller's registers, which control the I/O pins.

For example, in an **AVR microcontroller**, the code to turn on an LED connected to a specific pin might look like this:

```assembly
    ; Set PORTB0 to output
    SBI DDRB, 0         ; Set bit 0 of DDRB to 1
(output mode)

    ; Turn on LED connected to PORTB0
    SBI PORTB, 0        ; Set bit 0 of PORTB to 1 (LED
ON)
```

In this example, the SBI instruction sets specific bits in the **DDRB** and **PORTB** registers, which control the direction and value of pins on port B. By directly manipulating these registers, Assembly allows you to control the hardware with minimal overhead.

## FIRMWARE DEVELOPMENT AND BOOTLOADERS

Firmware is the software that provides low-level control over the embedded hardware. It often consists of a bootloader, which is the first piece of software that runs when a device is powered on. The bootloader is responsible for initializing the hardware and loading the main application into memory.

In many embedded systems, the bootloader is written in Assembly. Writing a bootloader in Assembly ensures that the system can start up as efficiently as possible, with minimal code size and fast execution. A typical bootloader might perform the following tasks:

1. **Initialize hardware peripherals**: Set up communication interfaces, memory, and timers.
2. **Load the main application**: the main program from non-volatile storage (like flash memory) into RAM.
3. **Jump to the application code**: After loading, the bootloader transfers control to the main program.

Writing a bootloader in Assembly is crucial for ensuring that the embedded system starts up quickly and can perform its intended tasks without delays or resource wastage.

# Operating System Kernel Development

## WRITING LOW-LEVEL OS COMPONENTS IN ASSEMBLY

Operating systems are the foundation of modern computing, managing hardware resources and providing essential services to programs. At the core of an operating system is the **kernel**, which handles low-level operations such as process scheduling, memory management, and hardware communication. Many operating systems are written in a combination of high-level languages (like C) and low-level Assembly, especially for performance-critical parts.

Assembly language plays a critical role in **OS kernel development**. The kernel must interact with hardware at a very low level, and in many cases, using Assembly is the most efficient way to achieve this. For instance, the kernel needs to manage **interrupts**, which are signals from hardware devices that require immediate attention.

Handling interrupts efficiently requires direct manipulation of hardware registers, and Assembly is ideal for this task.

A simple example of Assembly in an OS kernel might be handling an interrupt to switch between running processes. In x86 architecture, the interrupt handler might look like this:

assembly

```
; Interrupt handler entry point
PUSHAD                  ; Save all registers
MOV AX, 0x20            ; Load the interrupt vector
IN AL, 0x60             ; Read the interrupt status
; Perform context switch or other operations
POPAD                   ; Restore registers
IRET                    ; Return from interrupt
```

In this code, the PUSHAD and POPAD instructions are used to save and restore the state of the CPU's registers, which is crucial when handling interrupts. The MOV and IN instructions manipulate the CPU's registers to respond to the interrupt. This is a simple example, but it shows how Assembly is used to write performance-critical code in the kernel.

## LOW-LEVEL MEMORY MANAGEMENT

One of the most important tasks of an operating system kernel is **memory management**. The kernel must allocate and free memory, manage virtual memory, and handle memory protection. These tasks often require direct manipulation of the CPU's memory management unit (MMU) and page tables, which is typically done using Assembly.

For example, when the kernel needs to set up virtual memory, it directly manipulates the **page tables** and sets the necessary flags in the MMU registers. This level of control is only possible with

Assembly, as high-level languages cannot directly access hardware-specific features like the MMU.

assembly

```
    ; Set up page table entry
    MOV AX, [page_table]
    MOV BX, 0x1000      ; Set the physical address
    OR  BX, 0x001       ; Set the present flag in
the page table entry
    MOV [AX], BX        ; Write the value to the
page table
```

In this example, the kernel manipulates the page table entries directly, ensuring that virtual memory is mapped to the correct physical addresses. This low-level memory management is an essential part of operating systems, and Assembly provides the control needed to manage it efficiently.

# Reverse Engineering and Security

## USING ASSEMBLY TO ANALYZE AND BREAK DOWN SOFTWARE

Reverse engineering is the process of analyzing software to understand how it works or to uncover hidden features, vulnerabilities, or malware. Assembly language is a crucial tool for reverse engineers because it allows them to look at the raw machine code and see exactly what a program is doing at the lowest level.

When you reverse engineer a program, you are essentially deconstructing its machine code to understand its behavior. This is often done by disassembling the program, which converts the binary code back into Assembly. From there, the reverse engineer can analyze the code for specific functionality, vulnerabilities, or malware.

One of the key techniques in reverse engineering is **static analysis**, where you disassemble the binary and examine the resulting Assembly code to understand how the program works. For example, when analyzing a malicious piece of software, you might disassemble the code and look for unusual instructions or system calls that could indicate malicious behavior, such as accessing sensitive files or sending data over the network.

EXAMPLE OF REVERSE ENGINEERING USING ASSEMBLY

Here's an example of a simple disassembly process. Suppose you have a program that takes user input and performs some action. You want to analyze the program to see if it contains any hidden functionality.

1. **Disassemble the Program**: Use a disassembler like **IDA Pro** or **Ghidra** to convert the program's binary into Assembly code.
2. **Examine the Code**: Look for specific instructions or system calls that might indicate key operations, such as file access or network communication.
3. **Identify Vulnerabilities**: In many cases, reverse engineers are looking for vulnerabilities—places in the code where an attacker could inject malicious code. For example, buffer overflow vulnerabilities are often discovered by examining how the program handles input.

# Hands-On Project: Build a Simple Program for an Embedded System

Let's put the concepts of embedded systems into practice with a hands-on project. In this project, we'll write a simple program for an embedded system—a microcontroller that controls an LED. This program will read an input signal (like a button press) and turn the LED on or off based on the input.

## STEP 1: SETTING UP THE DEVELOPMENT ENVIRONMENT

For this project, we'll use an **AVR microcontroller**, which is commonly used in embedded systems. The microcontroller has several I/O pins that we can use to connect peripherals like LEDs, buttons, and sensors. You'll need to install the appropriate tools to work with AVR, such as **AVR-GCC** and **AVRDUDE** for compiling and uploading code to the microcontroller.

1. Install **AVR-GCC** for compiling Assembly and C code.
2. Install **AVRDUDE** for uploading the code to the microcontroller.

## STEP 2: WRITING THE CODE

The goal of the program is to turn on an LED when a button is pressed. Here's the Assembly code that will accomplish this:

```assembly
section .data
    button_pin db 0     ; Store button pin value (0 =
pressed, 1 = not pressed)

section .bss
    led_pin resb 1      ; Reserve memory space for
LED pin

section .text
    global _start

_start:
    ; Set the button pin as input (assume it's on
PORTB)
```

```
    SBI DDRB, 0              ; Set PORTB0 as input
(button)

    ; Set the LED pin as output (assume it's on
PORTC)
    SBI DDRC, 0              ; Set PORTC0 as output (LED)

    ; Check if the button is pressed
    IN  R16, PINB           ; Read input from PORTB
(button pin)
    AND R16, 1              ; Check if the button
(PORTB0) is pressed

    ; If the button is pressed, turn on the LED
    BREQ button_not_pressed
    SBI PORTC, 0            ; Set PORTC0 high (turn on
LED)
    JMP end_program

button_not_pressed:
    ; If the button is not pressed, turn off the LED
    CBI PORTC, 0            ; Set PORTC0 low (turn off
LED)

end_program:
    ; Infinite loop to keep the program running
    JMP end_program
```

## STEP 3: COMPILE AND UPLOAD THE CODE

1. **Assemble the Code**: Use **AVR-GCC** to assemble the
   program:

   bash

   ```
   avr-gcc -mmcu=atmega328p -o program.elf
   program.asm
   ```

2. **Upload the Code**: Use **AVRDUDE** to upload the program to
   the microcontroller:

```bash
bash

avrdude -c usbasp -p m328p -U
flash:w:program.elf:i
```

3. **Test the Program**: Once the program is uploaded to the microcontroller, you can test it by pressing the button. When the button is pressed, the LED should turn on; otherwise, it should stay off.

## Conclusion

In this chapter, we explored the real-world applications of Assembly language in several critical areas of modern computing, including **embedded systems**, **operating system kernel development**, and **reverse engineering**. Assembly continues to play a crucial role in low-level software development, offering unmatched control over hardware and optimizing system performance.

We also went through a hands-on project to build a simple program for an embedded system. This practical exercise gave you experience with writing Assembly code for microcontrollers, interacting with hardware directly, and optimizing memory and performance in a resource-constrained environment.

By mastering the concepts and techniques in this chapter, you'll be better equipped to apply Assembly programming in real-world scenarios, whether you're working with embedded systems, low-level system software, or analyzing existing software for vulnerabilities.

# CHAPTER 10: WORKING WITH INTERRUPTS AND I/O OPERATIONS

In the world of low-level programming, particularly in embedded systems and real-time systems, **interrupts** and **I/O operations** play a crucial role in ensuring that the system responds quickly and efficiently to external events. Whether it's handling user input, managing hardware communication, or responding to time-critical tasks, interrupts are a key feature that allows software to interact with hardware in a non-blocking manner.

In this chapter, we will delve deep into **interrupts**, explore their role in real-time systems, and understand how they are managed. We'll also look at **I/O operations**, particularly focusing on techniques like **Direct Memory Access (DMA)**, which improves the speed and efficiency of data transfers between memory and peripherals. Finally, we'll walk through a hands-on project where you'll write an Assembly program to handle an I/O device using interrupts and DMA techniques.

## Interrupts and Their Role in Real-Time Systems

### WHAT IS AN INTERRUPT?

An **interrupt** is a mechanism that allows a program to temporarily halt its current execution to address an external event or condition. The interrupt can come from either **hardware** or **software**, and its primary function is to provide a way for the CPU to respond to real-time events, such as I/O requests, sensor inputs, or timer events, without having to constantly check for those events within the main program flow.

In a typical system, the CPU follows a sequence of instructions until it completes a task. However, when an interrupt occurs, the CPU temporarily suspends its current operations to execute an **interrupt handler** or **interrupt service routine (ISR)**, which is a small function that handles the interrupt. Once the ISR is completed, the CPU resumes its previous operations, picking up where it left off.

Interrupts are particularly important in **real-time systems**, where timely responses to external events are critical. For instance, in systems such as automotive control systems, robotics, and medical devices, failure to respond to an interrupt could result in catastrophic consequences. Interrupts ensure that high-priority tasks, like handling sensor data or responding to user input, are addressed promptly.

## HARDWARE INTERRUPTS

Hardware interrupts are generated by hardware components such as I/O devices (keyboards, mice, sensors) or system timers. When these devices need the CPU's attention, they send an interrupt signal to the processor. The interrupt controller, which is part of the CPU, processes these signals and triggers the appropriate ISR.

Common examples of hardware interrupts include:

- **Timer interrupts**: These interrupts occur at regular intervals, typically used in systems that need to execute tasks at specific time intervals.

- **I/O device interrupts**: When a peripheral device (like a keyboard, mouse, or network card) requires CPU attention, it sends a hardware interrupt. For example, when data is ready to be read from a disk or when a button is pressed on a controller.

When a hardware interrupt is triggered, the CPU pauses its current operation, saves its state, and jumps to the corresponding ISR to handle the event. The CPU then restores its state and continues executing the program.

## SOFTWARE INTERRUPTS

Software interrupts, unlike hardware interrupts, are triggered by software instructions rather than external hardware events. A software interrupt is typically used for system calls, where a program requests a service from the operating system. In Assembly, a software interrupt can be triggered using specific instructions like the INT instruction.

An example of a software interrupt is the system call in Linux. When a program needs to interact with the operating system, like reading from a file or allocating memory, it can trigger a software interrupt, which causes the CPU to call the operating system's kernel functions.

For example, in x86 Assembly:

```assembly
mov eax, 4          ; sys_write system call number
mov ebx, 1          ; File descriptor 1 (stdout)
mov ecx, message    ; Address of the message to write
mov edx, 13         ; Length of the message
int 0x80            ; Call the kernel
```

In this example, the `int 0x80` instruction triggers a software interrupt, which invokes the `sys_write` system call to write a message to the screen.

In real-time systems, managing interrupts is crucial to ensure that the system responds to critical events in a timely manner. Interrupts must be handled quickly to prevent the system from missing any important signals.

The **priority of interrupts** is an important consideration. In many systems, interrupts are categorized by priority, ensuring that more critical events are addressed first. For instance, a timer interrupt that keeps track of real-time clocks may have higher priority than a peripheral interrupt that reads data from a sensor.

Some systems also use **interrupt masking**, where certain interrupts are temporarily disabled to prevent them from interfering with the execution of higher-priority tasks. Interrupt nesting, where one interrupt can interrupt another interrupt, is also a technique used in real-time systems to ensure that high-priority tasks are never blocked.

# Managing I/O Operations

I/O operations involve the transfer of data between the CPU and peripheral devices. These operations are typically slower than CPU processing, so efficient handling of I/O is crucial to system performance. I/O operations can be managed in several ways, including **polling**, **interrupts**, and **Direct Memory Access (DMA)**.

## POLLING VS. INTERRUPTS

**Polling** is a technique where the CPU continually checks (or "polls") a device to see if it needs attention. While polling is simple, it is inefficient because the CPU spends time checking devices even when they don't need attention, wasting precious processing cycles.

In contrast, **interrupts** allow the CPU to continue executing tasks and only respond when a device signals that it requires attention. This is far more efficient, as the CPU does not waste time checking devices that are not active.

However, interrupts are not always suitable for all types of I/O operations, especially when the system needs to handle a large number of devices or high-speed data transfers. This is where **Direct Memory Access (DMA)** comes in.

## DIRECT MEMORY ACCESS (DMA)

**Direct Memory Access (DMA)** is a technique that allows peripherals to directly read from and write to the system's memory without involving the CPU. This bypasses the CPU for data transfer, which can greatly improve the efficiency of I/O operations, especially in systems with large amounts of data transfer.

DMA is commonly used for operations like reading data from a disk or streaming audio from a device. The DMA controller is a dedicated hardware component that handles these data transfers independently of the CPU. Once the data transfer is complete, the DMA controller sends an interrupt to the CPU to inform it that the operation has finished.

The key advantage of DMA is that it frees up the CPU to perform other tasks while data is being transferred in the background. This leads to significant improvements in system performance, particularly in systems that need to handle large amounts of data in real-time.

### *Example of DMA in Action*

Let's say you have a system where data is being read from a sensor and needs to be stored in memory. Without DMA, the CPU would need to read the data from the sensor, process it, and then store it in memory. With DMA, the sensor can directly transfer its data to the memory, allowing the CPU to focus on other tasks.

## USING DMA IN ASSEMBLY

In Assembly, configuring and using DMA typically involves directly interacting with the **DMA controller registers**. For example, in a typical DMA operation, you would need to:

1.  Set the source address (where the data is coming from).
2.  Set the destination address (where the data should be written in memory).
3.  Configure the size of the data transfer.
4.  Enable the DMA controller to begin the transfer.

Here's a simplified example in Assembly pseudocode for setting up a DMA transfer:

```
assembly

; Configure DMA channel
MOV DMA_SRC, 0x1000      ; Set source address to
0x1000
```

```
MOV DMA_DST, 0x2000       ; Set destination address to
0x2000
MOV DMA_SIZE, 1024        ; Set data size to 1024
bytes

; Start the DMA transfer
MOV DMA_CTRL, 1           ; Enable DMA
WAIT_FOR_DMA_DONE:
    CMP DMA_STATUS, 0     ; Check if DMA transfer is
complete
    JE WAIT_FOR_DMA_DONE  ; Wait until transfer is
done

; DMA transfer completed, handle next operation
```

This code configures the DMA transfer, waits for the operation to complete, and then proceeds with further tasks once the data has been transferred.

# Hands-On Project: Writing an Assembly Program to Handle an I/O Device

Now that we've covered the theory of interrupts, I/O operations, and DMA, let's move on to a hands-on project. In this project, we will write an Assembly program that interacts with an I/O device—a simple **LED** connected to a microcontroller. We'll use interrupts to handle user input (via a button) and turn the LED on or off based on that input.

### STEP 1: SET UP THE DEVELOPMENT ENVIRONMENT

To complete this project, you'll need to set up your development environment with the appropriate tools for working with microcontrollers. For this example, we will use an **AVR microcontroller** with the **AVR-GCC** toolchain and **AVRDUDE** for uploading the code to the microcontroller.

1. Install **AVR-GCC** to compile your code.
2. Install **AVRDUDE** for uploading the program to the microcontroller.

## STEP 2: WRITING THE ASSEMBLY CODE

The goal of this project is to read input from a button, use an interrupt to handle the button press, and toggle an LED on or off based on that input. The program will use the **INT0 interrupt** for the button press and handle the LED on **PORTB**.

```
assembly

section .data
    led_on db 1         ; LED ON
    led_off db 0        ; LED OFF

section .bss
    button_press resb 1  ; Reserved space for button
press state

section .text
    global _start

_start:
    ; Initialize PORTB for output (LED control)
    SBI DDRB, 0         ; Set PORTB0 as output (LED)

    ; Initialize INT0 interrupt for button press
    SBI GICR, INT0      ; Enable INT0 interrupt
    SBI MCUCR, ISC01    ; Trigger interrupt on
falling edge (button press)

    ; Main loop
main_loop:
    JMP main_loop       ; Infinite loop to keep the
program running

; Interrupt Service Routine for INT0 (button press)
int0_isr:
```

```
    ; Read the button press
    IN  R16, PINB       ; Read the state of the
button (PORTB0)
    TEST R16, 1         ; Check if button is pressed
(low)
    JZ button_released  ; If button is not pressed,
skip toggle

    ; Toggle LED on PORTB0
    IN  R16, PORTB      ; Read current LED state
    XOR R16, 1          ; Toggle LED state
    OUT PORTB, R16      ; Write new LED state to
PORTB

button_released:
    RETI                ; Return from interrupt
```

In this code:

- We set up **PORTB0** as an output to control the LED.
- We configure **INT0** to trigger on a falling edge (button press) and jump to the interrupt service routine (int0_isr).
- The ISR checks the button press and toggles the LED accordingly.

STEP 3: COMPILE AND UPLOAD THE CODE

1. **Assemble the Code**: Use **AVR-GCC** to compile the Assembly code:

   bash

   ```
   avr-gcc -mmcu=atmega328p -o program.elf
   program.asm
   ```

2. **Upload the Program**: Use **AVRDUDE** to upload the code to the microcontroller:

   bash

```
avrdude -c usbasp -p m328p -U
flash:w:program.elf:i
```

3. **Test the Program**: After uploading the program to the microcontroller, pressing the button should toggle the LED on and off.

## Conclusion

In this chapter, we covered essential concepts related to **interrupts** and **I/O operations**, which are foundational in real-time systems and embedded systems development. We explored how interrupts are used to respond to external events, the importance of managing I/O operations efficiently, and how **Direct Memory Access (DMA)** improves data transfer speeds. Additionally, we learned how to write Assembly programs that interact with hardware using interrupts.

Through the hands-on project, you gained practical experience writing an Assembly program that handles an I/O device using interrupts, a critical skill for working with embedded systems. By understanding and leveraging interrupts and I/O operations, you're well-equipped to write low-level code for performance-critical applications.

# CHAPTER 11: USING ASSEMBLY FOR SYSTEM-LEVEL PROGRAMMING

System-level programming is a critical aspect of low-level computing, where software directly interacts with the underlying hardware or the operating system (OS). While high-level programming languages give developers the ability to create applications with ease, system-level programming allows us to write software that can interact directly with the OS, manage hardware resources, and implement low-level services. At the heart of this lies **Assembly language**, which offers unparalleled control over the hardware and system resources.

In this chapter, we'll explore how Assembly can be used for system-level programming. We'll cover topics such as making **system calls** in Assembly, **interfacing with the operating system**, and the role of Assembly in **writing device drivers**. Additionally, we'll walk through a hands-on project where you will write an Assembly program to interact with an OS API, reinforcing these concepts through practical application.

By the end of this chapter, you will gain a solid understanding of how Assembly is used in system-level programming, and you will have the hands-on skills to write low-level programs that interface with the OS and hardware.

# System Calls and Interface with the Operating System

A **system call** is a mechanism that allows a program to request services from the operating system. When you write a program in a high-level language, it often relies on the operating system for tasks like reading files, allocating memory, or managing processes. These services are provided by the OS and can only be accessed via system calls.

In Assembly, interacting with the operating system often involves making system calls directly. Each operating system provides a set of predefined system calls that can be invoked from user-level programs. For example, in Linux, system calls such as `read()`, `write()`, `exit()`, and `fork()` provide essential services for interacting with files, processes, and the system environment.

To make a system call in Assembly, you typically place the system call number (which identifies the specific service being requested) into a register, along with any arguments (e.g., a file descriptor or memory address). You then invoke a special instruction, like `int 0x80` on x86 Linux systems, which triggers the system call and passes control to the OS.

## SYSTEM CALLS IN LINUX (X86 ARCHITECTURE)

In Linux (on x86 architecture), system calls are made using the `int 0x80` instruction. This triggers a software interrupt, which the OS intercepts to execute the requested service. The system call number is placed in the **EAX register**, and any additional arguments are placed in other registers like **EBX**, **ECX**, and **EDX**.

For example, to write data to the console using the `sys_write` system call, you would do the following in Assembly:

```assembly
section .data
    msg db 'Hello, world!', 0xA  ; The message to
print

section .text
    global _start

_start:
    ; Write system call (sys_write)
    mov eax, 4                  ; sys_write system call
number
    mov ebx, 1                  ; File descriptor 1
(stdout)
    mov ecx, msg                ; Pointer to the
message
    mov edx, 14                 ; Length of the message
    int 0x80                    ; Trigger interrupt to
make the system call

    ; Exit system call (sys_exit)
    mov eax, 1                  ; sys_exit system call
number
    xor ebx, ebx                ; Exit status 0
    int 0x80                    ; Trigger interrupt to
make the system call
```

In this code:

- `mov eax, 4` places the system call number for `sys_write` in the **EAX** register.
- `mov ebx, 1` specifies the file descriptor for standard output (stdout).
- `mov ecx, msg` loads the address of the message into the **ECX** register.
- `mov edx, 14` sets the length of the message to be written.

- Finally, `int 0x80` makes the system call to write the message to stdout.

The second part of the code makes a `sys_exit` system call to terminate the program with an exit status of 0.

In Windows, system calls are made through a different mechanism called **Windows API**. Unlike Linux, where `int 0x80` is used for system calls, Windows applications typically use the **Windows API** to make system calls. The system calls themselves are implemented in dynamic link libraries (DLLs), like **kernel32.dll**.

However, in a lower-level context like Assembly, you can still make system calls by interfacing directly with the Windows system's underlying mechanisms. For example, you might use **INT 0x2E** or other methods specific to the version of Windows you are targeting. For simplicity, most Windows system-level programming in Assembly is done via the API functions, where you call a function from a DLL using a function pointer.

# Writing and Debugging Drivers

## THE ROLE OF ASSEMBLY IN CREATING DEVICE DRIVERS

A **device driver** is a piece of software that enables an operating system to communicate with hardware devices. These drivers are responsible for handling specific devices, such as printers, network adapters, hard drives, and more. Assembly language plays a crucial role in writing device drivers because it allows developers to interact directly with the hardware.

While most modern device drivers are written in **C or C++**, Assembly is still used in certain critical sections where performance is paramount or where low-level hardware access is required. For example, drivers for embedded systems, custom peripherals, or real-time applications may involve Assembly to achieve optimal performance.

## HOW ASSEMBLY IS USED IN WRITING DEVICE DRIVERS

Device drivers typically perform tasks such as:

1. **Initializing hardware**: Setting up control registers, configuring interrupt handlers, and enabling the device for operation.
2. **Handling interrupts**: Responding to events generated by hardware devices and managing the interrupt vectors.
3. **Transferring data**: Reading from or writing to memory buffers that store data being sent to or received from hardware.

In Assembly, writing device drivers often involves directly manipulating hardware registers and memory-mapped I/O. For instance, controlling the read/write operations of a hard disk or configuring a network card involves working directly with the device's hardware registers, which can be more efficiently done in Assembly.

## EXAMPLE OF AN ASSEMBLY DRIVER CODE FOR AN I/O PORT

Consider the task of writing a simple device driver that interacts with an I/O port. In this example, we'll simulate reading data from a port and processing it. Here's a snippet of Assembly code for interacting with an I/O port:

```assembly
assembly

section .data
    port_address db 0x60   ; I/O port address

section .text
    global _start

_start:
    ; Read a byte of data from the I/O port
    mov al, [port_address]    ; Move the data from the
I/O port to the AL register

    ; Perform some action with the data
    ; (e.g., process the byte of data)

    ; Exit the program
    mov eax, 1                      ; sys_exit system call
number
    xor ebx, ebx                   ; Exit status 0
    int 0x80                       ; Make the system call
```

In this code:

- The program reads data from the I/O port at address `0x60`.
- It moves the data from the port to the **AL** register, where further processing can occur.
- The program then exits using a system call.

## DEBUGGING DEVICE DRIVERS IN ASSEMBLY

Debugging device drivers, especially in Assembly, can be tricky because you're working directly with hardware. Here are some common techniques used in debugging:

1. **Using Debugging Tools**: Tools like **GDB** (GNU Debugger) and **WinDbg** (Windows Debugger) can help you step through driver code and inspect memory, registers, and I/O ports.

2. **Printing Debug Information**: For device drivers, you might use a debug output function to print messages or register values, which helps in understanding the flow of execution.
3. **Simulating Hardware**: In many cases, you can simulate the hardware or use a virtual machine to test the driver without requiring the actual hardware device.

# Hands-On Project: Write an Assembly Program to Interact with an Operating System API

Now that we understand system calls, device drivers, and debugging techniques, let's move on to a hands-on project. In this project, we'll write a simple Assembly program to interact with an OS API. Specifically, we will write a program to use the `sys_write` system call in Linux to write a string to the console.

### STEP 1: SET UP THE ENVIRONMENT

1. Install **NASM** (Netwide Assembler) for compiling Assembly code:

   bash

   ```
   sudo apt install nasm
   ```

2. Install **LD** (GNU linker) for linking object files:

   bash

   ```
   sudo apt install binutils
   ```

3. Install **GDB** (GNU Debugger) for debugging:

   bash

```
sudo apt install gdb
```

## STEP 2: WRITING THE ASSEMBLY CODE

Create an Assembly file named `hello.asm` that uses the **sys_write** system call to print a string to the console.

```assembly
assembly

section .data
    msg db 'Hello, Assembly!', 0xA  ; Message to
print with newline

section .text
    global _start

_start:
    ; sys_write system call
    mov eax, 4                ; sys_write system call
number
    mov ebx, 1                ; File descriptor 1
(stdout)
    mov ecx, msg              ; Pointer to the
message
    mov edx, 15               ; Length of the message
(including newline)
    int 0x80                  ; Trigger interrupt to
make the system call

    ; sys_exit system call
    mov eax, 1                ; sys_exit system call
number
    xor ebx, ebx              ; Exit status 0
    int 0x80                  ; Trigger interrupt to
make the system call
```

This program will print "Hello, Assembly!" to the console using the `sys_write` system call.

1. **Assemble the Code**:

   bash

   ```
   nasm -f elf32 hello.asm -o hello.o
   ```

2. **Link the Object File**:

   bash

   ```
   ld -m elf_i386 -s -o hello hello.o
   ```

3. **Run the Program**:

   bash

   ```
   ./hello
   ```

This will print `Hello, Assembly!` to the console.

## STEP 4: DEBUGGING WITH GDB

To debug the program, you can use **GDB** to step through the instructions and inspect the register values.

1. Start GDB with the following command:

   bash

   ```
   gdb ./hello
   ```

2. Set a breakpoint at the start of the program:

   bash

```
(gdb) break _start
```

3. Run the program:

```bash
(gdb) run
```

4. Step through the instructions to observe the register values:

```bash
(gdb) step
(gdb) info registers
```

## Conclusion

In this chapter, we explored the fundamental concepts of **system-level programming** using Assembly. We learned about **system calls** and how to interface with the OS, focusing on Linux system calls like `sys_write`. We also discussed the role of Assembly in **writing device drivers**, where we interact directly with hardware through low-level instructions.

By writing an Assembly program to interact with the OS API, you gained practical experience in using system calls and working with Assembly to perform I/O operations. With these skills, you're now equipped to write low-level programs that interact directly with the operating system and hardware, and to debug these programs using tools like GDB.

# CHAPTER 12: PERFORMANCE TUNING AND BENCHMARKS

Performance tuning is an essential part of low-level programming, particularly in environments where hardware resources like CPU speed, memory, and I/O throughput are constrained. When working with Assembly language, where you have fine-grained control over the hardware, optimizing code for performance can have a dramatic impact on the overall speed and efficiency of your programs. This chapter will guide you through the process of **identifying performance bottlenecks**, utilizing **benchmarking tools and techniques**, and implementing **performance benchmarks** in Assembly to test and optimize your code.

The ability to write fast and efficient code is a crucial skill, especially in embedded systems, real-time applications, and performance-critical software. By the end of this chapter, you'll be equipped with the knowledge and practical skills to analyze, measure, and optimize the performance of your Assembly programs, ensuring they run as quickly and efficiently as possible.

## Identifying Performance Bottlenecks

### What is a Bottleneck?

In computing, a **bottleneck** refers to any part of a system that limits the overall performance due to its lower speed or capacity compared to the other parts of the system. In the context of software, a performance bottleneck is the section of the program that consumes the most time or resources, causing the entire program to run slower than expected.

When working with Assembly, the bottlenecks are often caused by inefficient code or suboptimal hardware interaction. These bottlenecks could be related to memory access, inefficient algorithms, or poor use of CPU instructions. Identifying these bottlenecks is the first step toward optimizing the performance of your program.

## How to Identify Bottlenecks in Assembly Code

1. **Understand the CPU's Execution Model**: Before diving into optimizing code, it's crucial to understand how the CPU executes instructions. Modern CPUs feature **pipelining, out-of-order execution**, and **parallelism**. Each instruction goes through stages like fetching, decoding, executing, and storing. Some instructions, such as **multiplication** and **division**, take more time to execute compared to simpler ones like **addition** or **bitwise operations**.

   Understanding the CPU's execution model will allow you to identify which instructions are causing delays. For example, using **division** or **floating-point operations** instead of simple **integer operations** could introduce performance slowdowns.

2. **Analyze Memory Access Patterns**: Accessing memory is much slower than accessing CPU registers. The most efficient programs minimize memory accesses by keeping data in registers as much as possible. **Cache misses** (when the data is not available in the CPU cache and needs to be fetched from slower memory) can significantly slow down performance.

By optimizing memory access patterns, such as by using **sequential memory accesses** rather than **random accesses**, you can ensure that the CPU cache is used effectively.

3.  **Look for Redundant Instructions**: In Assembly, small inefficiencies can add up. For instance, performing the same computation multiple times or storing the same value in memory repeatedly can result in unnecessary operations. Carefully examine your code for opportunities to eliminate redundancy.
4.  **Use Efficient Algorithms**: The choice of algorithm can have a significant impact on performance. An inefficient algorithm can easily become the largest bottleneck in your code. Assembly programming gives you direct control over how data is processed, so choosing the right algorithm and optimizing it for the hardware is crucial.

    For example, an algorithm with **O(n^2)** time complexity, like **bubble sort**, might be acceptable for small datasets but could cause performance issues with larger inputs. Opting for algorithms with better time complexity, like **quick sort** or **merge sort**, will lead to better performance in larger systems.

5.  **Utilize Profiling Tools**: Profiling tools allow you to measure where your code spends the most time and identify the performance bottlenecks. Tools like **gprof** or **perf** can provide detailed insights into function-level performance, showing you how much CPU time each function consumes and helping you identify parts of the code that need optimization.

- **Memory Access Bottlenecks**: Excessive memory reads and writes, especially to slower types of memory like RAM, can be a major performance issue. Using registers more effectively and optimizing memory access patterns can help mitigate this.
- **Inefficient Looping**: Loops that iterate unnecessarily or contain redundant instructions inside can cause significant delays. Optimizing loops to minimize their execution time is essential.
- **Instruction-Level Bottlenecks**: Some instructions, like division or floating-point operations, take more CPU cycles to execute. Replacing expensive operations with cheaper ones can significantly boost performance.

# Benchmarking Tools and Techniques

### WHY BENCHMARK?

Benchmarking is the process of measuring the performance of a system or application to identify its strengths and weaknesses. In Assembly programming, benchmarking allows you to measure the time it takes for specific parts of the code to execute, which helps you identify performance bottlenecks and areas for optimization.

By running benchmarks, you can directly measure the effects of optimization changes and ensure that your program is running as efficiently as possible.

## TIME METRICS

One of the most basic metrics for benchmarking performance is **execution time**—the amount of time it takes for a program or a specific section of code to run. Measuring execution time can help you identify how long a program takes to perform a certain task and how long it takes to complete a full iteration of the program.

### *Measuring Time in Assembly*

To measure execution time in Assembly, you can use the **RDTSC** instruction (Read Time-Stamp Counter) on x86 processors, which returns the number of CPU cycles since the system was powered on. This instruction allows you to measure the time taken by a block of code in terms of CPU cycles.

Here's an example of how to use **RDTSC** to measure the time of an operation:

```assembly
    ; Start measuring time
    rdtsc                    ; Store the current time-
stamp in EDX:EAX

    ; Your code to benchmark (e.g., a loop or
function)
    ; Some operation, like a loop or a calculation

    ; End measuring time
    rdtsc                    ; Get the time-stamp again
    sub edx, [start_time]    ; Subtract the start time
from the end time
    sub eax, [start_time]
    ; Now EAX contains the number of cycles taken for
the operation
```

This code stores the start and end time-stamp values in the **EAX** and **EDX** registers, and the difference between them gives you the number of CPU cycles taken by the code block.

## CACHE PERFORMANCE METRICS

Modern CPUs have several levels of cache (L1, L2, L3) to speed up memory accesses. When your program makes inefficient memory accesses, it can result in **cache misses**, which slow down performance. By using benchmarking tools, you can measure cache hits and misses to optimize your program's memory usage.

### *Using perf for Cache Performance*

In Linux, the **perf** tool can be used to measure cache performance. Running a command like this can show you the number of cache misses:

```bash

perf stat -e cache-misses ./my_program
```

This command runs the program and reports the number of cache misses, which helps you identify inefficient memory access patterns that could be causing performance issues.

## CPU CYCLE METRICS

CPU cycles refer to the number of clock cycles the CPU uses to execute instructions. Reducing the number of cycles spent on each instruction is crucial for high-performance programming. You can measure the number of CPU cycles consumed by your code using **RDTSC**, as shown previously, or use profiling tools like **gprof** to track the CPU time consumed by each function in your program.

# Hands-On Project: Implement a Performance Benchmark for an Assembly Function

In this project, we will implement a simple performance benchmark for an Assembly function. The goal is to measure the execution time of a function that performs a mathematical operation, and then optimize that function to reduce the time it takes to execute.

Let's start by writing a simple function that calculates the sum of the squares of the numbers from 1 to N.

```assembly
section .data
    N equ 1000000          ; Number of iterations

section .text
    global _start

_start:
    ; Start measuring time
    rdtsc                  ; Get start time
    mov esi, 1             ; Initialize counter to 1
    mov ecx, N             ; Set loop limit to N
    xor eax, eax          ; Clear the result
register

loop_start:
    ; Calculate square of the current number
    imul ebx, esi, esi    ; Multiply counter by
itself (square the number)
    add eax, ebx          ; Add the square to the
total sum
    inc esi               ; Increment the counter
    loop loop_start       ; Repeat until counter
reaches N
```

```
    ; End measuring time
    rdtsc                      ; Get end time
    sub edx, [start_time]   ; Subtract start time from
end time
    sub eax, [start_time]   ; Result is in EAX (in
terms of CPU cycles)

    ; Output the result (number of cycles)
    ; Your output code goes here (e.g., print the
result)
```

This function calculates the sum of squares for the numbers from 1 to N, using a loop to iterate through each number and adding its square to the running total. The RDTSC instructions at the beginning and end of the program measure the CPU cycles taken by the function.

## STEP 2: RUN THE BENCHMARK

Assemble and run the code to measure the time it takes to execute the function:

1. **Assemble the Code**:

   bash

   ```
   nasm -f elf64 my_benchmark.asm -o
   my_benchmark.o
   ```

2. **Link the Object File**:

   bash

   ```
   ld -o my_benchmark my_benchmark.o
   ```

3. **Run the Program**:

```
bash

./my_benchmark
```

This will print the number of CPU cycles taken to compute the sum of squares.

## STEP 3: OPTIMIZE THE CODE

Now that we have a baseline, let's try optimizing the code to reduce the number of CPU cycles. One way to optimize this is by using **vectorization**, where possible, or minimizing the number of instructions executed per iteration.

For example, we can eliminate redundant operations, combine instructions, or adjust the loop to reduce unnecessary operations:

```assembly
; Optimized version of the sum of squares calculation
section .data
    N equ 1000000

section .text
    global _start

_start:
    ; Start measuring time
    rdtsc
    mov esi, 1
    mov ecx, N
    xor eax, eax

optimized_loop:
    ; Use SIMD or other techniques to optimize the
loop here
    imul ebx, esi, esi
    add eax, ebx
    inc esi
```

```
loop optimized_loop

; End measuring time
rdtsc
sub edx, [start_time]
sub eax, [start_time]

; Output result
; Your output code goes here
```

This optimization might involve removing unnecessary register manipulations, using more efficient multiplication techniques, or finding opportunities to reduce branching in the loop.

### STEP 4: RE-BENCHMARK AND COMPARE

After making changes, recompile and rerun the benchmark to compare the results. You should observe a reduction in CPU cycles, indicating that the optimizations have had a positive impact on performance.

## Conclusion

In this chapter, we've covered essential techniques for **performance tuning** and **benchmarking** Assembly code. We started by identifying performance bottlenecks in Assembly, such as inefficient memory access patterns, redundant instructions, and poor algorithm choices. Then, we explored various **benchmarking tools and techniques**, including **execution time metrics**, **cache performance**, and **CPU cycle counting**. Finally, we walked through a hands-on project, where we wrote a performance benchmark, optimized the code, and measured the results.

Performance tuning in Assembly requires a deep understanding of how the CPU operates, the memory system works, and how instructions execute at the hardware level. By applying these concepts and techniques, you can write faster, more efficient Assembly programs that make the most of available system resources.

# CHAPTER 13: EXPLORING ADVANCED MACHINE CODE

Machine code is the lowest-level language a computer can execute, consisting of binary instructions that the CPU directly understands. While Assembly allows programmers to write human-readable code that gets translated into machine code, diving deeper into **advanced machine code** optimizations can lead to significant performance improvements, especially when working with different processor architectures and specialized hardware features.

In this chapter, we will explore advanced techniques for optimizing code at the machine level. We'll cover how to write **Assembly** code that's tailored for specific processor architectures, such as **ARM**, **x86**, and **RISC**. We'll also discuss the importance of **SIMD** (Single Instruction, Multiple Data) and how to leverage **parallelism** and **vectorization** to improve the performance of your programs on multi-core CPUs. Finally, we'll work on a hands-on project where we'll write optimized code using **SIMD instructions**.

By the end of this chapter, you'll have a solid understanding of how machine code interacts with various CPU architectures and how to write highly efficient, architecture-specific Assembly code. You will also gain practical experience in utilizing **SIMD** for parallel processing.

# Optimizing for Specific Architectures

To optimize code for different processor architectures, you need to understand how each processor works internally. The key differences between processor architectures affect how Assembly code is executed, how instructions are fetched and processed, and how memory is accessed. The most common processor architectures today are **x86**, **ARM**, and **RISC**-based processors, each of which has its unique characteristics and optimization opportunities.

## ASSEMBLY FOR X86 PROCESSORS

The **x86** architecture, originally developed by Intel, is one of the most widely used processor families for general-purpose computing, especially in personal computers, laptops, and servers. x86 processors are known for their rich instruction set, complex pipelining, and support for both 32-bit (x86) and 64-bit (x86-64) operations.

The x86 architecture includes a wide range of instructions, including **complex arithmetic operations**, **multimedia instructions**, and **floating-point operations**. These instructions are highly optimized for tasks like integer arithmetic, logic operations, and system calls. However, to achieve maximum performance, you need to understand how to write code that minimizes pipeline stalls and makes efficient use of registers.

### *Optimizing x86 Assembly Code*

1. **Minimize Instruction Latency**: x86 processors feature **out-of-order execution**, meaning that instructions can be executed in parallel if there are no dependencies. However, some instructions are inherently slower than others (e.g., division is slower than addition). Therefore, the best practice is to order your instructions to avoid stalls and keep the CPU's pipeline filled with useful instructions.
2. **Leverage SSE and AVX**: x86 processors support **SIMD** instructions through the **SSE** (Streaming SIMD Extensions) and **AVX** (Advanced Vector Extensions) instruction sets. These instructions allow you to process multiple data points simultaneously, making them ideal for tasks like graphics processing, signal processing, and scientific computations.
3. **Use Registers Efficiently**: The x86 architecture includes a small set of general-purpose registers (e.g., EAX, EBX, ECX), and efficient use of these registers can reduce the need for memory access, which is much slower than register manipulation.

## ASSEMBLY FOR ARM PROCESSORS

ARM (Advanced RISC Machines) processors are widely used in mobile devices, embedded systems, and increasingly in desktops and servers. ARM is based on a **RISC** (Reduced Instruction Set Computing) architecture, which emphasizes simplicity and efficiency in its instruction set. ARM processors are designed to execute instructions with fewer cycles, enabling low power consumption while maintaining high performance.

ARM processors are particularly dominant in mobile devices, including smartphones, tablets, and IoT devices, thanks to their efficiency and low power requirements.

### *Optimizing ARM Assembly Code*

1. **Use ARM's Load/Store Architecture**: ARM uses a **load/store architecture**, meaning that operations are only performed on registers and memory accesses must be done explicitly. Understanding this principle is crucial for optimizing ARM Assembly code.
2. **Leverage NEON and SIMD**: ARM processors support the **NEON** SIMD extension, which allows for vectorized operations, similar to SSE and AVX on x86 processors. NEON is highly optimized for multimedia applications, including video processing, audio encoding/decoding, and machine learning tasks.
3. **Optimize for Low Power Consumption**: ARM processors are often used in power-sensitive devices, so optimizing code for low power consumption is critical. This involves minimizing the number of instructions and memory accesses, as well as using low-power states of the CPU.

## ASSEMBLY FOR RISC PROCESSORS

**RISC** processors, as the name suggests, use a **Reduced Instruction Set** compared to **CISC** (Complex Instruction Set Computing) architectures like x86. The RISC approach focuses on simplicity, using instructions that are all roughly the same length and that can execute in a single clock cycle.

While RISC is typically used in specialized processors, such as **SPARC**, **MIPS**, and **PowerPC**, the principles of RISC apply to ARM as well. RISC processors typically offer better performance per watt compared to CISC processors due to their simpler instruction set.

1. **Leverage Simple Instructions**: RISC processors typically have simple, uniform instructions. While this makes RISC code easy to write, it also means that complex operations may need to be broken down into multiple simple instructions. Efficient RISC programming involves reducing the number of instructions per operation.
2. **Register Usage**: RISC processors have a larger number of general-purpose registers compared to x86. Maximizing register usage is crucial for reducing memory access, which can be slow.
3. **Use Branch Prediction**: Like other processors, RISC processors use branch prediction to optimize instruction pipelines. Minimizing branch instructions, particularly in tight loops, can prevent pipeline stalls and improve performance.

# Understanding SIMD and Parallelism

## WHAT IS SIMD?

**SIMD (Single Instruction, Multiple Data)** is a parallel computing technique that allows the CPU to process multiple data elements simultaneously with a single instruction. This is particularly useful for tasks that involve large amounts of data that can be processed independently, such as image processing, scientific computations, and cryptography.

SIMD operations work by executing the same operation on multiple pieces of data at once. For example, adding two arrays of numbers can be done in a single SIMD instruction instead of performing individual additions for each element.

Modern processors, including x86 and ARM, include SIMD extensions (such as **SSE, AVX**, and **NEON**) that enable SIMD operations. These extensions allow the CPU to operate on multiple pieces of data in parallel, significantly speeding up operations that would otherwise be performed sequentially.

## How SIMD Improves Performance

SIMD improves performance by increasing the throughput of operations. Instead of processing one data element at a time, SIMD allows you to process multiple elements in parallel, effectively reducing the time taken to perform tasks on large datasets.

For example, if you want to add two arrays of 4 integers, with traditional scalar operations, you would need 4 separate instructions, each adding one pair of integers. With SIMD, the CPU can process all 4 integers in a single instruction, reducing the number of operations and the total time required.

## Parallelism in Modern CPUs

Modern CPUs, especially those designed for high-performance computing, feature **multi-core architectures**, where each core can execute instructions independently. Parallelism involves splitting tasks into smaller chunks that can be executed concurrently on different cores. This allows programs to run faster by utilizing all available CPU cores.

In Assembly, leveraging parallelism typically involves writing code that can be executed in parallel across multiple cores, or using SIMD instructions to process data in parallel within a single core.

# Hands-On Project: Write Optimized Code Using SIMD Instructions

In this hands-on project, we will write an Assembly program to perform a common data processing task—**vector addition**—using SIMD instructions. The goal is to demonstrate how SIMD instructions can be used to process multiple data elements in parallel, resulting in improved performance.

## Step 1: Setting Up the Environment

1. **For x86 SIMD (SSE/AVX)**:
   - o Install **NASM** (Netwide Assembler) to compile Assembly code:

     bash

     ```
     sudo apt install nasm
     ```

   - o Install **GCC** (GNU Compiler Collection) for linking the object file:

     bash

     ```
     sudo apt install gcc
     ```

2. **For ARM SIMD (NEON)**:
   - o Install **ARM GCC** toolchain:

     bash

     ```
     sudo apt install gcc-arm-none-eabi
     ```

   - o Install **QEMU** (for ARM emulation) to run and test the code.

# Step 2: Writing the SIMD Code

We will implement SIMD vector addition using **SSE** (Streaming SIMD Extensions) for x86 processors. This involves adding two arrays of 4 floating-point numbers in parallel.

Here's how you can write SIMD vector addition using **SSE** in Assembly:

```assembly
assembly

section .data
    array1  dd 1.0, 2.0, 3.0, 4.0   ; Array 1 with 4
elements
    array2  dd 5.0, 6.0, 7.0, 8.0   ; Array 2 with 4
elements
    result  dd 0.0, 0.0, 0.0, 0.0   ; Result array to
store the sum

section .text
    global _start

_start:
    ; Load array1 into xmm0 register
    movaps xmm0, [array1]

    ; Load array2 into xmm1 register
    movaps xmm1, [array2]

    ; Add the arrays (xmm0 + xmm1) and store the
result in xmm0
    addps xmm0, xmm1

    ; Store the result from xmm0 into the result
array
    movaps [result], xmm0

    ; Exit the program
    mov eax, 60             ; sys_exit system call
    xor edi, edi           ; Exit status 0
    syscall
```

1. **Assemble the Code**:

```bash

nasm -f elf64 -o vector_add.o vector_add.asm
```

2. **Link the Object File**:

```bash

gcc -nostartfiles -o vector_add vector_add.o
```

3. **Run the Program**:

```bash

./vector_add
```

This program adds two arrays of 4 floating-point numbers in parallel using **SSE instructions**. The `movaps` instruction loads packed single-precision floating-point values into the **xmm0** and **xmm1** registers. The `addps` instruction performs the addition in parallel for all 4 elements of the arrays. The result is then stored back into the `result` array.

## STEP 4: ANALYZE AND OPTIMIZE THE CODE

To analyze the performance of the SIMD-optimized code, you can use profiling tools like **perf** or **gprof** to measure the execution time and compare it with a non-SIMD version of the program. This will help you see how much performance improvement you've achieved by leveraging SIMD.

To implement SIMD vector addition on ARM using the **NEON** extension, the approach is similar but requires using ARM-specific instructions.

1. Write the ARM SIMD code using **VMUL** (vector multiply) or **VADD** (vector add).
2. Compile and link the program using the ARM toolchain.
3. Run the code on an ARM emulator or a physical ARM device.

## Conclusion

In this chapter, we explored how **advanced machine code optimizations** can be applied to various processor architectures, including **x86**, **ARM**, and **RISC**. We learned how to optimize Assembly code for each architecture, focusing on efficient use of registers, SIMD instructions, and memory access patterns. We also delved into **SIMD** and **parallelism**, explaining how these technologies enable programs to process multiple data elements simultaneously, resulting in significant performance gains.

Through the hands-on project, we implemented SIMD vector addition using **SSE** for x86 processors and saw how to optimize a program using **SIMD instructions**. The knowledge gained from this chapter equips you with the tools to write efficient, architecture-specific Assembly code that can take full advantage of modern hardware capabilities, making your programs faster and more scalable.

# CHAPTER 14: ADVANCED ALGORITHMS IN ASSEMBLY

In the world of low-level programming, implementing efficient algorithms and data structures is a powerful skill. Assembly language, with its direct control over the hardware, offers the opportunity to optimize algorithms to an extraordinary level of performance. While high-level languages offer abstracted data structures and built-in sorting algorithms, Assembly requires us to implement everything manually. In this chapter, we will dive deep into **advanced algorithms** and **data structures** in Assembly, covering how to implement everything from basic data structures like linked lists and hash tables to complex algorithms like **quicksort** and **RSA encryption**.

By the end of this chapter, you will understand how to work with fundamental data structures and advanced algorithms in Assembly. You will also have the hands-on experience of writing an optimized sorting algorithm that will highlight the power of low-level optimizations.

## Data Structures in Assembly

Data structures are the backbone of algorithms, and how you organize your data significantly impacts the performance of your program. While high-level languages like Python, Java, or C++ have built-in data structures such as **arrays**, **linked lists**, and **hash tables**, in Assembly, we need to implement these data structures ourselves. However, this gives us complete control over memory usage and execution speed, allowing for highly optimized solutions.

## IMPLEMENTING ARRAYS IN ASSEMBLY

An **array** is a collection of elements stored in contiguous memory locations. Arrays are one of the simplest data structures and can be implemented easily in Assembly. In most cases, arrays are used to store lists of data, such as integers, strings, or even other arrays.

In Assembly, you can create an array by reserving memory in the **data section**. The size of the array is defined at compile time, and accessing elements is done by using offsets from the base address.

Here is an example of implementing and accessing an array in Assembly (using x86 Assembly):

```assembly
section .data
    ; Define an array with 5 integers
    arr db 1, 2, 3, 4, 5

section .text
    global _start

_start:
    ; Load the first element of the array into the AL
register
    mov al, [arr]     ; arr[0] -> AL register

    ; Add the second element to AL
    add al, [arr+1]   ; arr[1] -> AL register

    ; Exit program
    mov eax, 60       ; sys_exit system call
    xor ebx, ebx      ; Exit status 0
    syscall
```

In this example:

- We define an array `arr` with 5 elements in the **data section**.
- To access the first element, we use the offset `[arr]`, and to access the second element, we use `[arr + 1]`. The value is then loaded into the **AL** register, where it can be used for further operations.
- The `add` instruction then adds the second array element to the value in **AL**.

Arrays are often used as the building blocks for more complex data structures, such as linked lists and hash tables.

## IMPLEMENTING LINKED LISTS IN ASSEMBLY

A **linked list** is a collection of elements (called **nodes**), where each node contains two parts: the data and a pointer to the next node in the sequence. Linked lists allow dynamic memory allocation and are particularly useful when you don't know in advance how many elements you'll need to store.

In Assembly, implementing a linked list involves managing memory and pointers manually. Here's an example of how to implement a simple **singly linked list** with a few nodes:

```assembly
section .data
    ; Define node data for linked list
    node1_data db 10        ; Data for node 1
    node2_data db 20        ; Data for node 2
    node3_data db 30        ; Data for node 3

section .bss
    node1 resb 4   ; Reserve 4 bytes for node 1 (data
+ next pointer)
```

```
    node2 resb 4   ; Reserve 4 bytes for node 2 (data
+ next pointer)
    node3 resb 4   ; Reserve 4 bytes for node 3 (data
+ next pointer)

section .text
    global _start

_start:
    ; Initialize node 1
    mov byte [node1], 10       ; Data for node 1
    lea rdi, [node2]           ; Next pointer for
node 1 points to node 2
    mov [node1+1], rdi         ; Store pointer to
node 2 in node 1's "next" field

    ; Initialize node 2
    mov byte [node2], 20       ; Data for node 2
    lea rdi, [node3]           ; Next pointer for
node 2 points to node 3
    mov [node2+1], rdi         ; Store pointer to
node 3 in node 2's "next" field

    ; Initialize node 3
    mov byte [node3], 30       ; Data for node 3
    mov [node3+1], 0           ; Null pointer for the
next node

    ; Exit program
    mov eax, 60                ; sys_exit system call
    xor ebx, ebx               ; Exit status 0
    syscall
```

In this example:

- We define three nodes (node1, node2, and node3) in the **.bss** section, which allows us to reserve space for the nodes.
- Each node stores data (the first byte) and a pointer to the next node (the second byte, which is a memory address).

- The `lea` instruction is used to load the address of the next node into a register, and this address is stored in the next pointer of the current node.

The linked list can be traversed by following the pointers from one node to the next until the pointer is `null`, indicating the end of the list.

## IMPLEMENTING HASH TABLES IN ASSEMBLY

A **hash table** is a data structure that maps keys to values using a **hash function** to compute an index into an array of buckets or slots. Each slot in the array holds a list of values that share the same hash index. Hash tables are highly efficient for lookup, insertion, and deletion operations, with an average time complexity of **O(1)**.

In Assembly, implementing a hash table involves manually managing memory and handling collisions (when two keys hash to the same index). Here's a simplified example of how a hash table might be implemented in Assembly:

```
assembly

section .data
    keys db 1, 2, 3, 4         ; Keys to hash
    values db 10, 20, 30, 40   ; Values to store

section .bss
    hash_table resb 16         ; Reserve 16 bytes for
the hash table

section .text
    global _start

_start:
    ; Hash function (simplified for demonstration
purposes)
```

```
    ; Here we just take the key modulo 4 to get an
index
    mov al, [keys]              ; Load the first key
into AL
    mov ah, 4                   ; Modulo 4
    div ah                      ; AL / AH, result in AL
(index)

    ; Store the value in the hash table at the
computed index
    lea rdi, [hash_table]       ; Load address of hash
table
    mov bl, [values]            ; Load the first value
    mov [rdi+al], bl            ; Store the value in the
hash table slot

    ; Exit program
    mov eax, 60                 ; sys_exit system call
    xor ebx, ebx                ; Exit status 0
    syscall
```

In this example:

- The keys and values arrays hold the keys and values to be stored in the hash table.
- We use a **simple hash function** that calculates the index by taking the key modulo 4.
- The corresponding value is then stored in the hash table at the calculated index.

While this is a simplified example, it illustrates the basic idea of how a hash table works. In a real-world scenario, you'd implement collision resolution (such as chaining or open addressing) and a more complex hash function.

# Sorting, Searching, and Cryptography

## SORTING ALGORITHMS IN ASSEMBLY

Sorting is one of the most fundamental tasks in computer science, and many algorithms have been developed to sort data efficiently. Common sorting algorithms include **quick sort**, **merge sort**, **bubble sort**, and **insertion sort**. Implementing these algorithms in Assembly requires careful management of memory and registers, as Assembly gives you fine-grained control over the data manipulation process.

### *Quicksort in Assembly*

Quicksort is an efficient, comparison-based sorting algorithm with an average time complexity of **O(n log n)**. Here is a high-level overview of the quicksort algorithm:

1. Pick a **pivot** element from the array.
2. Partition the array into two subarrays: elements smaller than the pivot and elements larger than the pivot.
3. Recursively apply the quicksort algorithm to the subarrays.

Here is an example of how **quicksort** can be implemented in Assembly:

```assembly
section .data
    array db 10, 7, 3, 9, 1, 5, 6  ; Array to sort

section .text
    global _start

_start:
```

```
    ; Quicksort algorithm implementation (pseudocode
for demonstration)
    ; Partition the array around the pivot
    ; Recurse on left and right subarrays
    ; (Details omitted for brevity)

    ; Exit program
    mov eax, 60                        ; sys_exit system
call
    xor ebx, ebx                       ; Exit status 0
    syscall
```

The quicksort implementation in Assembly would involve managing indices, swapping elements, and recursively sorting the subarrays using the stack.

## SEARCHING ALGORITHMS IN ASSEMBLY

Searching algorithms allow us to find an element in a collection of data. The simplest searching algorithm is **linear search**, where each element is checked one by one until the target is found. A more efficient search is **binary search**, which divides the search space in half with each iteration, making it much faster for sorted data.

### *Linear Search in Assembly*

Linear search checks each element in the array sequentially. Here's a simple linear search algorithm in Assembly:

```
assembly

section .data
    array db 1, 3, 5, 7, 9, 11  ; Array to search
    target db 7                      ; Target value to
find

section .text
    global _start
```

```
_start:
    ; Perform linear search
    lea rdi, [array]                    ; Load address of
the array
    mov al, [target]                    ; Load the target
value into AL
    mov rcx, 6                          ; Number of elements
in the array

search_loop:
    cmp al, [rdi]                       ; Compare target
with the current array element
    je found                            ; If found, jump to
found
    inc rdi                             ; Move to the next
element in the array
    dec rcx                             ; Decrement the
counter
    jnz search_loop                     ; If not done,
continue the loop

not_found:
    ; Target not found, exit
    mov eax, 60                         ; sys_exit system
call
    xor ebx, ebx                        ; Exit status 0
    syscall

found:
    ; Target found, exit
    mov eax, 60                         ; sys_exit system
call
    xor ebx, ebx                        ; Exit status 0
    syscall
```

This code performs a **linear search** by iterating through the array and comparing each element with the target value.

## CRYPTOGRAPHY IN ASSEMBLY

Cryptography is a vital field that secures communications and protects sensitive data. One of the fundamental algorithms in cryptography is **RSA encryption**, a public-key cryptosystem that is widely used for secure data transmission.

### *RSA Encryption in Assembly*

RSA encryption involves large integer arithmetic, specifically modular exponentiation. While implementing RSA from scratch in Assembly is complex, it's an essential exercise for understanding how cryptography works at the machine level.

The general steps in RSA encryption are:

1. **Key Generation**: Generate a public and private key pair.
2. **Encryption**: Encrypt the plaintext using the public key.
3. **Decryption**: Decrypt the ciphertext using the private key.

Implementing RSA in Assembly would involve handling large numbers (bigger than the CPU registers can hold), performing modular exponentiation, and managing the cryptographic keys efficiently.

Here's an overview of the **RSA encryption** algorithm:

assembly

```
; RSA algorithm in Assembly
; 1. Key generation (public and private keys)
; 2. Modular exponentiation
; 3. Encryption using public key
; 4. Decryption using private key

; (Code implementation omitted for brevity)
```

# Hands-On Project: Write an Assembly Program for a Fast Sorting Algorithm

In this hands-on project, we will write an Assembly program to implement an optimized sorting algorithm. Specifically, we will implement **quicksort**, one of the most efficient sorting algorithms.

## STEP 1: SET UP THE DEVELOPMENT ENVIRONMENT

1.  Install **NASM** (Netwide Assembler) to compile the code:

    bash

    ```
    sudo apt install nasm
    ```

2.  Install **GCC** (GNU Compiler Collection) for linking:

    bash

    ```
    sudo apt install gcc
    ```

## STEP 2: WRITING THE QUICKSORT ALGORITHM

In this example, we will write an Assembly version of quicksort that works on an array of integers. We'll first implement the partition step, which rearranges the array around a pivot element, and then recursively sort the left and right subarrays.

assembly

```
section .data
    array db 10, 7, 3, 9, 1, 5, 6  ; Array to sort

section .text
    global _start
```

```
_start:
    ; Quicksort implementation
    ; Partition and recursive calls omitted for
brevity

    ; Exit program
    mov eax, 60                    ; sys_exit system
call
    xor ebx, ebx                   ; Exit status 0
    syscall
```

## STEP 3: COMPILE, LINK, AND RUN

1. **Assemble the Code:**

   ```bash
   nasm -f elf64 quicksort.asm -o quicksort.o
   ```

2. **Link the Object File:**

   ```bash
   gcc -nostartfiles -o quicksort quicksort.o
   ```

3. **Run the Program:**

   ```bash
   ./quicksort
   ```

## STEP 4: OPTIMIZE THE CODE

After running the program, analyze the performance and identify areas where you can reduce the number of instructions, minimize memory accesses, and make the algorithm more efficient.

## Conclusion

In this chapter, we explored advanced algorithms and data structures in Assembly. We covered essential data structures like arrays, linked lists, and hash tables, and discussed how to implement them manually in Assembly. We also delved into advanced algorithms like **quicksort** and **RSA encryption**, learning how to implement them at the machine level for better performance and control.

Through the hands-on project, you gained practical experience implementing a sorting algorithm in Assembly, showcasing the power of low-level programming. By mastering these techniques, you're well-equipped to handle complex algorithmic tasks with the precision and efficiency that Assembly offers.

# CHAPTER 15: FUTURE TRENDS AND ASSEMBLY LANGUAGE IN MODERN COMPUTING

As the field of computing continues to evolve at an unprecedented pace, new technologies and advancements are reshaping the way we think about programming and system optimization. **Artificial Intelligence (AI)** and **Machine Learning (ML)** are revolutionizing performance optimization and system automation. Meanwhile, the emerging field of **Quantum Computing** is challenging traditional computing paradigms, raising questions about how low-level programming languages, such as Assembly, will fit into the future of computing. In this chapter, we will explore the impact of AI and ML on low-level programming, investigate the role of Assembly in quantum computing, and guide you through a hands-on project that combines low-level programming with quantum computing concepts.

By the end of this chapter, you will gain insights into how Assembly is being used in modern computing and how it will continue to play a key role in future technologies like AI and quantum computing. You will also have the opportunity to experiment with creating an Assembly-based **simulator** that introduces you to basic concepts of quantum computing.

# The Impact of AI and Machine Learning on Low-Level Programming

Artificial Intelligence (AI) and Machine Learning (ML) are often seen as high-level applications that operate abstractly above the hardware layer. However, their influence on performance optimization in low-level programming is undeniable. With the increasing complexity of AI models, optimizing the hardware that runs these models has become just as critical as optimizing the software. As systems continue to evolve, the demand for **real-time, high-performance computing** (HPC) in AI applications has forced low-level programmers to reconsider how they write Assembly code.

AI models, particularly those in fields like deep learning, rely on massive amounts of data and require the ability to process that data quickly and efficiently. Achieving these efficiencies often demands optimizing the code running on GPUs, CPUs, and specialized processors like TPUs (Tensor Processing Units). Assembly language, with its close proximity to the hardware, is often used to fine-tune the behavior of these processors, ensuring that AI and ML models run with maximum efficiency.

## *AI and Hardware Optimization*

1. **Optimizing the GPU for Deep Learning**: Graphics Processing Units (GPUs) are crucial for AI workloads because they can perform many operations simultaneously. The architecture of GPUs relies heavily on **SIMD** (Single Instruction, Multiple Data) and **SIMT** (Single Instruction, Multiple Threads) execution models to process data in parallel. Assembly language can be used to directly control GPU resources for optimal performance. Writing Assembly

code for GPUs involves leveraging instruction sets like **CUDA** and **OpenCL**, which offer low-level access to the GPU's parallel execution capabilities. Optimizing kernel code in Assembly ensures that deep learning models run faster, training times are reduced, and power consumption is minimized.

2. **Optimizing AI Algorithms with Assembly**: AI and ML algorithms often require frequent matrix multiplications, convolutions, and other data-heavy operations. Assembly language allows developers to optimize these operations by controlling how data is loaded into registers, minimizing cache misses, and leveraging SIMD or vector instructions that operate on multiple data points simultaneously. By optimizing these operations at the Assembly level, performance can be dramatically improved. For example, in **matrix multiplication**, an essential operation in neural networks, writing Assembly code that optimizes memory access and computational efficiency can speed up the process by an order of magnitude.

3. **Low-Level Optimization of Neural Networks**: Neural networks are built upon layers of mathematical operations, which are computationally expensive. Assembly language allows for optimizing specific operations at the hardware level, ensuring that the most critical components of the neural network—like the **activation functions** and **backpropagation algorithms**—run efficiently. Additionally, Assembly can be used to control the **pipelining** of data, reducing latency and improving throughput.

## AI-DRIVEN COMPILERS AND ASSEMBLY OPTIMIZATION

As AI continues to advance, we are also seeing the rise of **AI-driven compilers** that can automatically optimize high-level code to run efficiently on specific hardware. These compilers use machine learning techniques to identify bottlenecks in code and apply performance improvements by generating optimized Assembly code for the target architecture.

- **Auto-tuning**: AI-driven compilers can learn from previous code execution patterns and use machine learning techniques to tune algorithms for optimal performance on specific hardware platforms. By analyzing execution patterns, the compiler can make decisions about instruction reordering, loop unrolling, or memory access optimizations that were previously done manually in Assembly.
- **Performance Prediction**: AI systems can predict the performance of different code optimizations by running simulations based on historical performance data. This allows developers to receive recommendations about the best Assembly-level optimizations to apply, saving time and increasing overall efficiency.

While these AI tools provide powerful optimization capabilities, the role of low-level programming in ensuring efficiency is still crucial. Understanding Assembly and how it interacts with modern AI workloads allows developers to have more control over the performance of AI applications, especially when optimizations are required at the hardware level.

# Assembly Language in Quantum Computing

## WHAT IS QUANTUM COMPUTING?

Quantum computing is a rapidly emerging field that harnesses the principles of quantum mechanics to solve problems that are currently intractable for classical computers. Unlike classical bits, which represent data as either 0 or 1, quantum bits (or **qubits**) can exist in a superposition of both 0 and 1 simultaneously, allowing quantum computers to process a vast amount of data in parallel.

Quantum computing has the potential to revolutionize fields such as cryptography, material science, pharmaceuticals, and complex simulations. However, programming quantum computers is vastly different from traditional computing, as it involves manipulating quantum states and understanding quantum gates.

## THE ROLE OF ASSEMBLY IN QUANTUM SYSTEMS

While quantum computing is still in its early stages, Assembly language plays an important role in understanding how low-level code can interact with quantum systems. Unlike traditional programming, where Assembly gives you direct control over registers and memory, Assembly for quantum computing requires working with **quantum gates** and **quantum states**.

Quantum computers are typically programmed using specialized languages like **QASM** (Quantum Assembly Language) or **Quipper**, which describe operations on qubits in terms of quantum gates. These quantum gates manipulate qubits by altering their quantum states. Although quantum programming is different from classical programming, the principles of **low-level control** and **optimization** remain important.

Assembly in quantum computing is essential for optimizing quantum circuits, particularly in **quantum error correction** and the efficient use of quantum gates. Quantum operations require precise timing and synchronization to ensure that the qubits interact correctly, making low-level programming vital for achieving maximum performance.

1. **Quantum Gates and States**: In quantum computing, **quantum gates** are used to perform operations on qubits, similar to how classical gates (like AND, OR, and NOT) operate on classical bits. These gates manipulate the **quantum state** of the qubits. Assembly code for quantum computing might involve specifying a sequence of quantum gates to transform a set of qubits from one state to another.
2. **Quantum Circuits**: A **quantum circuit** is a sequence of quantum gates applied to a set of qubits. In Assembly for quantum computing, you might be tasked with creating a sequence of gates that will perform a specific computation or simulation. Quantum circuits need to be optimized to minimize the number of gates and reduce the likelihood of errors, which are inherent in quantum systems.
3. **Quantum Error Correction**: One of the key challenges in quantum computing is **quantum decoherence** and **quantum noise**, which can corrupt quantum states during computation. Assembly programming for quantum computing includes implementing **quantum error correction** techniques, which add redundancy to quantum systems to prevent errors from propagating.

## CREATING AN ASSEMBLY-BASED SIMULATOR FOR QUANTUM COMPUTING CONCEPTS

Given the complexity of quantum computing hardware and the fact that quantum computers are not yet widely available, developing quantum simulators has become a common practice. A quantum simulator allows developers to simulate the behavior of qubits and quantum circuits on classical hardware. In this hands-on project, we will write an Assembly-based simulator for quantum computing concepts, which will introduce us to the basics of quantum state manipulation and quantum gates.

# Hands-On Project: Creating an Assembly-Based Simulator for Quantum Computing Concepts

In this project, we will simulate a simple **quantum gate operation** on a single qubit. Specifically, we will implement the **Hadamard gate**, which creates a superposition state, in Assembly.

## STEP 1: UNDERSTANDING THE QUANTUM HADAMARD GATE

The **Hadamard gate (H)** is a fundamental quantum gate used to put a qubit into an equal superposition of 0 and 1. For a qubit in the state $|0\rangle$, applying the Hadamard gate produces the state:

$$H|0\rangle = \frac{1}{\sqrt{2}}( |0\rangle + |1\rangle )$$

Similarly, for a qubit in the state $|1\rangle$:

$$H|1\rangle = \frac{1}{\sqrt{2}}( |0\rangle - |1\rangle )$$

In this project, we will use Assembly to simulate this behavior by applying mathematical operations to represent the quantum states.

## STEP 2: SETTING UP THE SIMULATOR

In Assembly, we will represent the quantum states using **complex numbers**, since quantum states involve superpositions that are represented by complex amplitudes. We will simulate the Hadamard operation using basic arithmetic and floating-point operations.

Here's a simplified version of the code in **x86 Assembly** to simulate a quantum Hadamard gate on a qubit:

```assembly
assembly

section .data
    ; Define initial state (|0⟩)
    zero db 1.0, 0.0       ; 1.0 + 0.0i (real +
imaginary part)
    one db 0.0, 1.0        ; 0.0 + 1.0i (real +
imaginary part)

section .text
    global _start

_start:
    ; Apply Hadamard gate to |0⟩
    ; H|0⟩ = (1/√2)(|0⟩ + |1⟩)

    ; Calculate (1/√2)(|0⟩ + |1⟩)
    ; For simplicity, we skip the 1/√2 normalization
here, focusing on the transformation.
    ; Add the amplitudes of |0⟩ and |1⟩.
    movsd xmm0, [zero]           ; Load the real part of
|0⟩
    movsd xmm1, [one]            ; Load the real part of
|1⟩
    addsd xmm0, xmm1             ; Add the real parts of
|0⟩ and |1⟩

    ; Store the result in a new state
    movsd [result_real], xmm0

    ; Exit program
    mov eax, 60                  ; sys_exit system call
    xor ebx, ebx                 ; Exit status 0
    syscall
```

In this code:

- We represent the qubits **|0⟩** and **|1⟩** as complex numbers.
- The Hadamard operation is applied by adding the real parts of the two qubit states and storing the result.

- The **xmm** registers are used to store floating-point values, and **addsd** performs the addition of the complex amplitudes.

## STEP 3: RUNNING THE SIMULATOR

1. **Assemble the Code**:

   bash

   ```
   nasm -f elf64 quantum_simulator.asm -o
   quantum_simulator.o
   ```

2. **Link the Object File**:

   bash

   ```
   gcc -nostartfiles -o quantum_simulator
   quantum_simulator.o
   ```

3. **Run the Program**:

   bash

   ```
   ./quantum_simulator
   ```

The result of this simulation would give you the transformed quantum state after applying the Hadamard gate to a qubit initially in the |0⟩ state.

## STEP 4: EXTENDING THE SIMULATOR

This basic simulator can be extended to support more quantum gates, like the **Pauli-X**, **Pauli-Y**, and **Pauli-Z** gates, or even multi-qubit operations such as **entanglement**. You could also add support for quantum measurements by collapsing the quantum state to a classical state, which could be implemented using random number generation to simulate the measurement outcome.

## Conclusion

In this chapter, we explored the fascinating intersection of **Assembly language** and **modern computing technologies** such as **AI**, **machine learning**, and **quantum computing**. We saw how **AI** is transforming low-level programming by driving hardware optimization, how **Assembly** remains relevant in the context of performance tuning for AI workloads, and how **quantum computing** presents new challenges and opportunities for low-level programmers.

Through the hands-on project, you learned how to write an **Assembly-based quantum simulator**, introducing you to the world of quantum programming at a very low level. While quantum computing is still in its infancy, the skills you've developed here can serve as a foundation for understanding and working with future quantum systems.

As we look ahead, **Assembly** will continue to play an essential role in **optimizing** algorithms, **interfacing with specialized hardware**, and even **simulating future computing systems** like quantum computers. The future of Assembly in modern computing is undoubtedly bright, as it remains a fundamental tool in understanding the inner workings of both classical and quantum systems.

# CONCLUSION: MASTERING HIGH-PERFORMANCE SYSTEMS WITH ASSEMBLY

Throughout this book, we've journeyed from the foundational elements of **Assembly programming** to exploring advanced techniques for optimizing and harnessing the full power of low-level system programming. We've covered everything from basic data structures and sorting algorithms to interfacing directly with hardware, and even delved into emerging technologies like quantum computing. If you've followed along, you now have the tools to write high-performance, efficient, and optimized code that interacts directly with hardware and software at a level of granularity most programmers rarely experience.

But this is just the beginning. Mastering **Assembly** is not just about writing code; it's about understanding how computers work at the most basic, atomic level. It's about pushing the boundaries of **performance**, fine-tuning algorithms, and optimizing systems in ways that allow software to run faster, smarter, and more efficiently. As you continue your journey with **Assembly programming**, you'll deepen your understanding of **computer architecture**, **low-level programming**, and the powerful relationship between hardware and software.

This concluding chapter will provide a recap of the key lessons we've learned throughout the book, offer advice on how to continue advancing your Assembly knowledge, and encourage you to keep pushing the boundaries of performance and innovation in the exciting world of low-level programming.

# Review of Key Concepts and Skills

Assembly programming requires a deep understanding of how the computer's hardware interacts with software. Unlike high-level programming languages, Assembly provides access to **CPU registers**, **memory**, and **input/output (I/O) devices**, giving you precise control over what the computer is doing at any given moment. As we've seen, this low-level control allows for significant performance optimization, making Assembly invaluable for situations where performance is paramount—such as in embedded systems, real-time computing, and performance-critical applications.

Throughout this book, we covered the following key concepts:

- **CPU Registers**: Registers are small, fast storage locations in the CPU used for storing data that the CPU is actively working with. We discussed how to use registers effectively, how to minimize memory access, and how to ensure that the CPU's processing capabilities are fully utilized.
- **Instruction Set**: Each processor has a specific set of instructions, called the **instruction set architecture (ISA)**. In this book, we explored popular ISAs, including **x86**, **ARM**, and **RISC**, and how each has its unique features, strengths, and considerations for optimization.
- **Memory Management**: We covered how data is stored and accessed in memory, from simple **arrays** and **linked lists** to more complex structures like **hash tables** and **binary trees**. Understanding how to efficiently manage memory—

minimizing access time and optimizing cache use—is critical for writing high-performance Assembly code.

- **System Calls and OS Interaction**: One of the most powerful aspects of Assembly is how it interacts with the operating system through **system calls**. We discussed how Assembly allows you to make low-level requests to the OS, such as reading and writing files, managing processes, and performing direct I/O operations.
- **Performance Optimization**: We explored how to analyze **performance bottlenecks**, use **profiling tools**, and apply **advanced techniques** like **SIMD** and **multi-core parallelism** to optimize your Assembly code for maximum efficiency. By leveraging hardware-specific features and optimizing data handling, you can ensure that your code runs as fast as possible.
- **Debugging and Troubleshooting**: Writing low-level code often requires precise debugging techniques. We covered how to use **debugging tools** like **GDB**, how to identify common issues in Assembly programs, and how to optimize your workflow for efficiency and accuracy.

## ADVANCED ALGORITHMS AND DATA STRUCTURES

One of the most exciting aspects of working with Assembly is implementing **advanced algorithms** and **data structures** manually. From implementing **linked lists** and **binary search trees** to applying **quicksort** and even implementing cryptographic algorithms like **RSA**, you've learned how to build and optimize algorithms from the ground up. In many cases, this hands-on experience with low-level data structures and algorithms can lead to a deeper understanding of how high-level programming languages implement these features behind the scenes.

Some of the algorithms and data structures we explored include:

- **Sorting Algorithms**: From **bubble sort** and **insertion sort** to **quicksort** and **merge sort**, you learned how to implement these algorithms in Assembly, paying careful attention to **memory usage, instruction cycles**, and **efficiency**.
- **Search Algorithms**: Whether it was **linear search** or **binary search**, you now understand how to apply these techniques directly in Assembly, optimizing for both time complexity and execution speed.
- **Cryptographic Algorithms**: Implementing cryptographic algorithms in Assembly, such as **RSA encryption**, allowed you to dive deep into how modern security algorithms work at the bit level, and how Assembly can be used to ensure that these algorithms run as efficiently as possible.
- **Data Structures**: By implementing core data structures like **arrays, linked lists, hash tables**, and **stacks**, you gained practical experience in managing data efficiently at the hardware level.

## SYSTEM-LEVEL PROGRAMMING WITH ASSEMBLY

One of the most critical skills we've covered in this book is writing **system-level programs** that interface directly with the operating system and hardware. Through **device drivers, interrupt handling**, and **low-level system calls**, you've learned how Assembly can be used to interact with hardware at the most fundamental level.

Key areas in system-level programming we covered include:

- **Interrupts**: Interrupts allow the CPU to respond to external events quickly without constantly checking for conditions. We covered how to work with hardware and software interrupts, and how to write **interrupt service routines** (ISRs) in Assembly to handle I/O operations, time-sensitive tasks, and external signals.

- **Input/Output (I/O)**: I/O operations in Assembly require interacting directly with the system's hardware. We discussed how **Direct Memory Access (DMA)** can optimize data transfer, and how Assembly is used to interface with I/O ports, memory-mapped devices, and external peripherals.
- **Writing Device Drivers**: Writing device drivers in Assembly is a critical skill in embedded systems and real-time systems. We looked at how to interact with hardware devices, manage memory, and handle device communication through low-level programming.
- **Operating System Interfaces**: Assembly is often used in writing low-level components of operating systems, such as **memory managers** and **process schedulers**. We explored how to make **system calls** to perform OS operations and how Assembly interacts with the kernel and hardware to manage system resources efficiently.

# Building on Your Assembly Knowledge

EXPANDING YOUR SKILLS WITH REAL-WORLD PROJECTS

Mastering Assembly is a continuous journey. Now that you have learned the foundational and advanced aspects of **low-level programming**, it's time to apply these concepts in real-world projects. Assembly programming, due to its close relationship with hardware, is often used in specific domains where performance is critical or where direct control of hardware is necessary. Here are a few areas where you can continue building your skills:

1. **Embedded Systems Development**: Assembly is the core language for programming embedded systems. Whether you're working with microcontrollers, IoT devices, or real-time systems, continuing to build projects in this space will deepen your understanding of how hardware and software interact. Projects like writing device drivers, managing

hardware resources, or optimizing sensor data processing can provide valuable experience.

2. **Performance-Critical Applications**: For high-performance applications, whether it's for scientific computing, video processing, or games, Assembly allows you to optimize code at the lowest level, making it faster and more efficient. Focus on optimizing algorithms, working with SIMD instructions, and using Assembly to target specific hardware like GPUs and FPGAs (Field-Programmable Gate Arrays).

3. **Operating System Development**: Operating systems rely heavily on low-level programming to manage hardware resources, memory, processes, and file systems. If you want to build your own operating system or contribute to existing ones, Assembly programming is essential. Work on projects that require implementing memory management, process scheduling, or writing system calls.

4. **Security and Cryptography**: The world of cryptography and cybersecurity often involves low-level programming. Implement cryptographic algorithms in Assembly to understand how modern encryption schemes work and how they can be optimized for speed and security. Consider building tools for **penetration testing** or **reverse engineering** software to better understand the vulnerabilities in modern systems.

5. **Simulators and Emulators**: One fascinating area of Assembly is building **simulators** and **emulators** for other processors or systems. This allows you to practice low-level systems programming and experiment with different architectures. You can simulate other CPU instruction sets, or even implement simple **quantum computing** simulators in Assembly.

One of the most exciting aspects of learning Assembly is the ability to push the boundaries of **performance**. Assembly gives you the power to write software that runs as efficiently as possible, making full use of the hardware's capabilities. However, it also requires a deep understanding of computer architecture, hardware, and low-level programming techniques.

As you continue your journey with Assembly, I encourage you to keep challenging yourself with increasingly complex projects. Whether it's implementing **real-time systems**, working with **multi-core processors**, or experimenting with **quantum computing**, there are endless possibilities for innovation and optimization.

## Encouragement for Future Learning

Assembly programming is not just about learning to write code at a low level; it's about understanding how computers work and how to **optimize performance** from the ground up. The skills you've learned in this book—whether it's working with **memory**, **hardware**, or **system calls**—will serve as a foundation for tackling any low-level programming challenge that comes your way.

Remember, the world of low-level programming is vast, and there's always more to learn. Don't be afraid to experiment, break things, and learn from your mistakes. The more projects you take on, the more you will uncover the true power of **Assembly** and the opportunities it provides for performance optimization.

## Final Thoughts

By mastering Assembly, you've acquired a powerful skill set that will set you apart as a programmer. You now understand how to write **high-performance** software that interacts with hardware, optimizes system resources, and pushes the boundaries of what's possible in modern computing. Keep building, keep experimenting, and keep learning. The journey into low-level programming has no limits, and with each new challenge, you'll continue to improve your ability to create efficient, fast, and innovative solutions.

As you continue to explore the evolving landscape of technology, remember that Assembly will remain a foundational tool in the world of computing. Whether you're optimizing for **AI**, developing the next generation of **embedded systems**, or diving into cutting-edge fields like **quantum computing**, Assembly programming will always be a critical skill for mastering high-performance systems. Happy coding!

www.ingramcontent.com/pod-product-compliance
Lightning Source LLC
LaVergne TN
LVHW022345060326

832902LV00022B/4265